May God Bless and keep you by His power!

Y. Sydell Dunn

A Journey: On Mighty Wings

Living, Dying, and Deliverance, Reflections of a Survivor

By:

T. Lydell Dunn

Foreword by:
Dr. Charles Portera, Jr.

WESTBOW
PRESS®
A DIVISION OF THOMAS NELSON
& ZONDERVAN

WestBow Press books may be ordered through booksellers or by contacting:

WestBow Press
A Division of Thomas Nelson & Zondervan
1663 Liberty Drive
Bloomington, IN 47403
www.westbowpress.com
1 (866) 928-1240

ISBN: 978-1-5127-3386-0 (sc)
ISBN: 978-1-5127-3385-3 (hc)
ISBN: 978-1-5127-3384-6 (e)

Library of Congress Control Number: 2016904080

Print information available on the last page.

WestBow Press rev. date: 3/24/2016

Table of Contents

Dedications

For the many, who have inspired and supported
me, as I have endeavored to complete this work
I want to say Thank You and I love you!

First of all, to my wife Bev. She is a "once in a lifetime" kind of
Love! She has endured much painful sacrifice through all of her
support for me, both in the sickness phase and the recovery phase.
She has provided invaluable help and support in helping me
throughout the past twenty-eight months to complete this work.

Our children, Justin, Tara, and Derrick have also supported me
all along the way, both in sickness and in health. I look forward
to having the time to reconnect and do some fun things.

Our many medical friends, too numerous to name that have
been so supportive throughout our illness and healing. Also,
for the support they provided in helping to bring about this
work. Although it may often go unrecognized, the care and
commitment provided by medical professionals everywhere
should be remembered. We would like to offer a special "Thank
You" to all those called to care for other human beings.

I also want to thank my work associates who were so gracious
in helping me to return to the job while giving me plenty of
space to re-remember all the things I had forgotten. It has been
a frustrating time for me, as I am sure it has been for you.

And finally, for our friends who assisted us with this document
by answering some of our questions or by helping us to correct
many of the errors made by a first time writer. There are way too
many to mention here but please know, I am eternally grateful.

I love you all, with all my heart!

Foreword

Rarely can it be said that one specific event changed the course of a man's life. However, what I witnessed on September 6th, 2013 did exactly that. In all of my experiences as a Surgical Oncologist who had basically grown up in the hospital environment, and as the son of a surgeon, I was totally blindsided by what I was witness to in a span of fifty-five minutes at the hospital where I practiced. That moment in time shook me to the core and left me with a whole new perspective on the presence of God in the world, the blessings of having a wonderful wife, children and family, and the calling to practice in the field of surgical oncology. When I came to work that fall day, I had no idea I would be leaving a different man….. forever changed.

I met Tony (Lydell) Dunn and his wife Beverly in my office in July of 2013. I reviewed with them Tony's diagnosis of pancreatic cancer while we went over the images of his CT and MRI scans. I described to them in detail the surgical procedure required to remove the cancerous mass: a major surgical operation known as the "Whipple Procedure." It is a radical and risky surgical procedure. It involves removal of the gallbladder and a portion of the bile duct, the head of the pancreas, the entire duodenum and one-third of the stomach; then reconnecting the common bile duct, pancreas and stomach that are then sewn, or connected, to the GI tract. I commented that Tony was not the typical patient, considering that all of the normal "outward signs" of cancer were absent. Nevertheless, there it was in black and white. Bev joked that she wasn't surprised I found Tony atypical. It was something she had known all along!

The day of surgery came, August 27, 2013 and the procedure was performed without incident. Tony progressed through the recovery phase for the next nine days. His recovery was fantastic with only a few minor hiccups along the way. He always met me with the same question as I came into his room, "When am I going home?" On the evening of the ninth day, I was surprised by his reluctance to go home when I had finally agreed he was ready to be discharged. For some reason Tony now had concerns about leaving the hospital. I found this strange but agreed to have him stay in the hospital for one more day. Later, we realized this interaction could very well have been the first of many events that helped to save his life.

The next morning my nurse, Deanna, prepared Tony's discharge orders. She would process Tony's release after attending an unexpected meeting. Her meeting that morning extended beyond its scheduled time by more than thirty minutes. During which time, Tony began to experience shortness of breath progressing into respiratory distress and followed by a cardiac arrest. A "Code Blue" was called. The resulting cardio-pulmonary arrest was due to a large saddle embolus (pulmonary embolus) that had lodged in both pulmonary arteries. I arrived in the MICU to witness as the code team executed all of the standard treatment options, administering more than three crash carts of medications and TPA which is not commonly administered in this setting so soon after a major abdominal surgery. All this, it seemed, to no avail. I observed at that time what I believed to be Tony's death. Tony had no cardiac electrical activity for over 55 minutes.

My mind now turned to breaking the devastating news to the family. As I left his room and walked toward the waiting room where the family and their friends had gathered, I saw them standing in a circle holding one another and praying to God. Something about the waiting room scene with all their sadness and grief arrested me. I could not go into the room to deliver the message that Tony was dying. I had walked on passed the door, escaping into the empty stairwell. There I questioned God's presence and reasoning for this event. I did not understand it at all! Why had this happened to such a wonderful, God-fearing man with such a loving and caring family? I cried out to God, "How can you do this? I've done everything I can do!" The operation went well, his recovery was going great, and now he was *dead*? I yelled at God, "What more do you want from me?" I had surrendered control and it was at that moment, I felt a warmness come over me from the inside out. Before, I had been cold and scared, but now I felt undeniable warmth and a sense of purpose. I am not certain of exactly what happened in that stairwell. All I can say is that I walked out a man who saw things differently. I have seen things differently ever since.

Shortly after returning to the MICU, I witnessed the semblance of a heartbeat on Tony's monitor and then the return of a regular heartbeat and blood pressure. Upon seeing this, my first sense was frustration. After going for (55) minutes without cardiac electrical activity, the chances of an anoxic brain injury due to no blood flow to his brain was high. What good would this man's life be if he lives the rest of his days in a vegetative state? Upon examination, I saw signs that he was indeed "in there"; he responded, he felt pain, and could interpret it and react to it much to my surprise.

I now found myself in a place I had never expected to ever be. What had happened? Had God been present in the treatment room? Had He heard the prayers that were prayed by his family? Had He heard the questions, doubts and anger expressed by me in the stairwell? The very fact that I was asking these questions meant that my spiritual world and understanding of God had been turned upside down. These are questions I would never have expected myself to be asking that day. But they are questions which continued to burn in my mind for many days to come. These questions are now changing who I am as a husband, a father, a son, brother and a physician. Most of all, they have changed me as a Christian.

I have realized as surely as Tony found new life that day, so did I. I now find myself looking for God in places I never thought He would be. I find myself loving those whom God placed in my life in a way I never knew I could love. I have found that I have a new compassion for those who come to me living out their own nightmares as they face down all the unknowns of a cancer diagnosis. I realize now that God is as BIG as I ever thought He was, but not so big that He can't visit one simple man at the hour of his greatest need. He is not too BIG to answer when a small band of believers cry out in an hour of desperation. I truly believe God is at His strongest when we are at our weakest. In one of my darkest hours as a surgeon I found a treasure of faith that will sustain me and impact all those I love for the rest of our days.

Dr. Charles Portera, Jr. MD
Surgical Oncology, General Surgery

**Dr. Portera, Jr. with Bev and me at
our "Gathering of Angels"**

A Journey to Somewhere Wonderful

"The soul is a divine gift imparted to every man by the Creator, and it is the driving force in all of us. Accepting this revelation is the first step in learning to successfully navigate this pathway on which we are placed." TLD

Photo: Beautiful Blarney Castle Gardens, Cork, Ireland. Taken 2004 used by Permission

Article One: My Long Journey Home

My mind was wandering as I sat in my study. It was Christmas, which is usually a time of deep reflection for me. I thought about my life, my family, and my friends. I was inspired and had to write!

During my lifetime, I have developed a deep reverence for the vastness and diversity of my Creator's world. Through the years, I have witnessed many things in many places. My journey has taken me thousands of miles. I have seen both wonderful and terrible things along the way. I have come to realize that my life has been made up of a series of travels. In actuality, it has been one solitary journey designed specifically for me. No one else will walk the exact same road because this is the pathway the Father has chosen to lead me Home. Every person will walk their own appointed pathway......all of which will lead to Home.

Through the years, I have chosen many places to call home. I have often pondered—why do we keep wandering? What is it we are seeking? Is our quest driven by our need for greater contentment or happiness? Do we seek security, stability, or peace in a life that is often full of danger and unpredictability? Are we just contentedly restless? We may not be aware that at the core of our being is a deep desire for significance and belonging. This desire inspires us to search for a place we have never been but know in our heart we need to go. A place we can call Home.

Our circumstances can play tricks on us from time to time. We get confused about where we really belong. Some respond to the hardships of life that have left them numb and empty, choosing a pathway of pleasures to fill their void. Others invest themselves in relationships that often result in despair and end in disappointment or betrayal. Others pursue beauty, power or control, and other elusive treasures to provide the self-worth they desperately crave.

They remain wanting. What they seek can only be found in a solitary place: Home.

What do we tell those who look in all the wrong places, always getting the wrong answers? Can they ever understand? They do not understand their longings because of their personal deprivation. Love, compassion, selflessness, and forgiveness are strangers to their hearts. These are things they have never known. They should experience these things in the safety of their earthly homes but in too many cases they have been deprived of this divine blessing. They know there is something better out there but they do not know what it looks like or how to attain it. Through courageous interventions, they must be shown by someone who cares for their soul. This new revelation is the light which brightens the path that leads them Home.

Many never realize that their humanity goes much deeper than what we see or feel. The unsearchable potential, in every person, is hidden deeply within their mind and spirit.....their soul. The soul is a divine gift imparted to every human being by the Creator. It is the driving life force in all of us. Accepting this revelation is the first step in learning to successfully navigate this pathway upon which we are placed. We are much more than just another animal. We are the crowning jewel of all creation. God made all of this for us. He has a purpose for every life. Accepting this truth propels us forward on a course leading directly toward Home.

Many theologians have told us that not all roads lead to God. To this, I beg to differ. All roads do indeed lead to God. He is the Alpha and Omega of every life. If we choose to deny God it will make no difference. Our destination will remain the same. Ultimately, every person will appear before Him. Every knee will bow before Him to acknowledge His supremacy. Many have accepted

Him superficially and then denied Him the intimate relationship He desires, leading to the same end.

There is no substitute for faith in God and reliance upon Him as Master. Those who deny this truth will one day find Home but will not have the key for gaining access and going inside. Those who receive the truth and bow in submission at His feet will be lifted up with His mighty hand. He will lead us through a life full of dangers, disappointments, and fears but He will deliver us from every evil by His power. Then He will lead us through His beautiful garden in sweet fellowship once again. His garden is the place we have been longing and searching for but have never been. This is the place God calls Home.

Written December 2012 – T. Lydell Dunn

After writing the previous passage, I felt a very troubled spirit. Was God warning me? Was death near? And then six months later I received a diagnosis: pancreatic cancer. I would have Radical surgery…..a "Code Blue" (with no heart beat for fifty-five minutes)…..and then a full recovery! Death was close but the life-giver was closer! I received a divine intervention and a miracle. God sustained me! For now, my journey continues…..

Social Media-Legacy of Prayer and Faith:

Posted: Beverly Rollins Dunn - July 23, 2013 Moon Shadows Tn.

Just to help catch such wonderful family and friends up-to-date with our unexpected journey, we will begin from Thursday to now. Tony thought he had pulled a muscle in his side when we played golf on vacation last month. The major pain subsided and he has had pain on and off since that mirrored classic symptoms of a bad gall bladder. He sought medical tx Thursday to get his GB checked. The GB was fine but they found a mass on the Pancreas on ultrasound. When he came home with news of a mass and a battle, the nurse knowledge in me went to my heart really quickly and I lost it..... his comment was "We are no different than anyone else". He just held me and let me cry, of which I did pretty much all night. My mind knew what a Pancreatic mass means, usually a very poor prognosis, and a short time and I just could not see my life here without him, and I just thought of everything from our kids and grandkids to our future plans, to our coming 20th anniversary in October. We laugh because Tony says as a nurse I was no support at all....LOL. Well, I was not a nurse at that point. I was a wife that was at a loss....... The comfort, as I moved through the past few days, from the Father, has surpassed my thoughts.....and then the support from our family and friends has been overwhelming. We are grateful to Dr. Swan and his office for starting us out on the right path and a special thank you to all my coworkers, a few by name, who let me cry as they listened to our news, tried to feed me, and above all prayed and gave me the word from our God by scripture and hugged and loved on me, when we were at Skyridge for our big tests. Suzanne Bynum, Carrie McAmis, Linda Triplett, Selina Rawls, Tricia Brockway, Jena Frederick, Gail Longwith, and Leia. Their support and likewise Tony's from Duracell, there are just no words. Thank you to Wanda Perry and Dr. Barrow from Skyridge, they will just never know. The results of the tests were better than we expected and they said if you could have cancer of the Pancreas, this was the kind to have and it is very slow growing.....We have an appointment with a surgical oncologist Monday in Chattanooga and have also had his records sent to MUSC for now. We request that you all pray for healing, guidance, strength, comfort, wisdom, and also great peace for not only us but especially our children.... And that I will be a supportive nurse....lol. I have become that since finding out the results, but I'm not sure he likes that now....FYI, nurses tend to be a little bossy and controlling.....but I love him dearly. Thank you all and remember us, and so many others, in prayer, that

face so many different battles and hardships that are much
greater than ours....

**Matthew 14:27 But immediately Jesus spoke to them,
saying, "Be of good cheer! It is I; Do not be afraid"
NKJV**

Article Two: The Reason I Write

At fifty-four years of age, I finally thought I knew where my life was heading.
In the not- too-distant future, I was anticipating a quiet retirement with
my beautiful bride and family. I was looking forward to the possibilities
of spending more time with the kids and grandkids and enjoying more of
the life we miss out on in this hurry-up world. Like so many others, much
of my time was spent working to pay the bills. I had dreams of what the
future would be when I could finally slow down and get out of the race.
Many thoughts filled my mind in those days, all of which were leading me
down a road to somewhere different.....somewhere wonderful!

In my thinking, I discovered a spiritually fatal flaw. As a Christian, I
had failed to stop and ask God if my plans, in actuality, were His plans.
I realized that my plans were not exactly His plans. I was unaware that
I was standing in need of a radical re-directing in my thought process. I
had lost track of my spiritual purpose and my understanding of just who
it is I serve and what it is He wants to accomplish with my life. I had no
idea what the Master had designed and planned for my immediate future.
His plan would radically regain my full attention and redirect my future
pathway entirely.

It is amazing what words such as cancer, pulmonary embolism, and
code blue can do to a person's thought process and psyche. Even more
poignant is seeing God's hand orchestrate these events. God did it in such
a way that it left everyone involved in absolute awe at what had taken
place. I was admitted to Memorial Hospital as an ordinary man in need
of healing. Thirty days later, (a little deviation from the eight to ten day
plan originally intended) I left Memorial Hospital as the "Miracle Man".
I had been affectionately labeled "Miracle Man" by my medical angels.
After all this time, the accounts of the medical professionals continue to

leave many of them in tears and me with cold chills, when we discuss the ordeal that unfolded.

As I write these words today, I do so having spent a great deal of time soul searching over the past several months, since being released from the hospital. My friends and family have encouraged me to write and share these events as well as the messages and enlightenments I have received as a result of it all. As I come today, trying to put everything into perspective, I have completed many different bits and pieces of this work. Since writing is a relatively new thing for me, I do so as I am inspired even if I do not know how it fits in the grand scheme of this work.

Hopefully, I will be able to arrange it in a way that makes sense and conveys the message that I think my Father (God) wishes me to convey. In my quest to understand exactly what happened, during those days when I was "clocked out" of life, I have asked many questions. I sought answers from my wife and family, my friends, and many new medical friend angels who were witness to the events surrounding my case. I will insert as many of their comments as possible, while respecting their privacy and professional obligations. It is really as much their story as it is mine.

This whole ordeal has been extremely unique for me. I have never been in a place where I was so totally dependent on everyone else to tell me things that intimately involved and relating directly to me. In all my questioning, I have come to realize that God chose and orchestrated this event to reach me with His message. God chose to use this event to reach many others who had various needs in their lives as well. I have been blessed by conversations with others, as through their tears, they have described the impact of what they witnessed and felt in those most difficult of hours and days. They continue to share what they have ultimately gleaned from their experience with my event. I find this to be the most amazing result of this story.

My purpose for writing is very clear. First of all, I want to lift up a sensationally awesome God who has power we cannot come close to imagining. He is beyond comprehending in all His works and ways. I want to leave a testimony to all my family and friends and whoever may end up reading this message about the impact of a divine visitation. It is my desire that these words will bring hope to others struggling with a recent diagnosis that has left them in shock and fearful despair. It is also my desire that it will be a help to those who may be struggling with any other hardship that is common to our human condition.

The hardships of this life are many and varied sometimes. I know first-hand that our God has the power to bring us through each and every trial we will ever face. He will do so with total victory, including the sweet victory over death. I will share with you some personal and spiritual reflections…..milestones in my life. I believe these have led and contributed to the divine intervention that we all have experienced. Through these reflections, on a broader scale, I want to attempt to reconcile these events to the scriptures. I wish to highlight the spiritual conditions existing in our personal lives, homes, churches, communities, nation, and our world. As minister of the gospel, I resubmit myself under the authority of God. I will complete the mission He has chosen for me, in much the same way that Jonah did after his deliverance from the belly of the fish.

We have planned a day of fellowship with our medical angels and loved ones, in what I have dubbed "A Gathering of The Angels." This is to celebrate the passing of one year of my new life. I do indeed feel that I have been born again and given a new opportunity. In fact, it was in preparation for this gathering that led me to the title for this book, "A Journey: On Mighty Wings; Living, Dying, and Deliverance, Reflections of a Survivor." I have absolutely no doubt that one year ago God gathered these individuals together for a special purpose. He brought us together to witness something amazing. This event would impact all of our lives in very special way. God used these individuals to initiate the needed physical healing in my life. More importantly, it has led to a spiritual healing and new direction for me, my family, and for many of them.

When scheduling the first anniversary gathering, we included a round of golf to the event. During my hospital stay, my wife Beverly promised our golfing caregivers that we would play a round when I had healed. Friday, September fifth, emerged as the day of our medical angel gathering and golf outing. Bev and I had to laugh when we realized the significance of this date. We were totally unaware it was actually the day before our "code blue" crash from one year earlier. In actuality, our celebration was the one year anniversary of my new life.

The date of the fifth and the number five is an extremely significant part of our entire story. It is just one example of the perfect divine order that has prevailed throughout this ordeal. The spiritual significance of the number five, the Hebrew letter Hei, as defined in Jewish writing and teaching has continued to amaze Bev and I throughout this whole miracle intervention. I will later share the relationship of the number five to the spiritual journey we have been traveling for the past several years, even before our medical miracle occurred. I was amazed to realize the spiritual significance when I began to search for God's divine purpose in what had happened. In hindsight, at least for Bev and I, it is just more evidence that the hand of God has been orchestrating this from the beginning.

Social Media- Legacy of Prayer and Faith:

Posted by: Beverly Rollins Dunn – August 5th, 2013 Moon Shadows Tn.

We are back home from Memorial with Tony. He feels pretty good but tired. We ask that you continue to pray, as we are hoping to find out all the results Friday. They biopsied some fluid from the Pancreatic cyst and actually said the cyst looked better than they thought. We just pray they have gotten enough fluid for adequate testing. The duct is still enlarged and blocked. They found a nodule on his esophagus, that we did not know was there, and they biopsied that also. Our immediate prayer is that he does not start in on Pancreatitis, as the pancreas is very twitchy and does not like to be touched. Pancreatitis is very painful and causes a great deal of nausea and vomiting. So, hopefully we will get everything and know our direction by Friday. Thank you all so much for the prayers, thoughts, kind words, and sweet friendships. We Love You!

1 Thess 5:16 Rejoice always, Pray without ceasing,…..NKJV

Starting our "Gathering of Angels" fellowship on the golf course was perfectly appropriate. This gathering was not only because many of our angels love the game or that Bev had promised them we would play golf when I was healed, more appropriately it was a round of golf that led to the initial diagnosis of pancreatic cancer. I'll explain later!

After our golf round, we gathered and shared a meal prepared by my dear friend and most favorite chef in the world, Chef Clyde Rush. He is not only a friend of the family but a huge blessing for his excellent culinary skills and service. He knows his stuff! Believe me, it is a culinary treat to be invited to his house for leftovers. An invitation from Chef Clyde is one you never want to turn down.

It is my sincere hope that this work will bring blessings to all who read these words. It is my hope that this brings comfort to the distressed and understanding to the confused. I hope it will bring conviction to the guilty in order to establish restoration of a relationship with the Creator. I want you to understand that salvation or deliverance comes to us through many different interventions. As we walk this road with Christ, this deliverance is both spiritual and physical.

To those who are unbelievers existing inside of the church, it is my hope this work brings the message of possibility. This condition of unbelief truly exist and on a very large scale. It is my prayer to impact the unbelievers outside of the church as well. One of the greatest realizations I have received is the astounding level of unbelief present in my own life. This comes as a result of a dependence on religion rather than relationship. To those who have not accepted the Christ of the Bible, Jesus of Nazareth, my prayer is that you will come to know Him. He is the one and only true source of life and He is waiting for you to come for your everlasting healing.

For now, many have asked about my current prognosis. I am happy to say that all of our most current checks and balances indicate we are cancer free. This is truly significant when one considers the statistics indicating that less than ten percent of those diagnosed with pancreatic cancer survive. The early, divinely guided diagnosis revealed malignant cancer cells in the earliest stages. So early in fact was my diagnosis, microscopic cancer cells were not fully detected upon analysis until after the defective specimen had been surgically removed.

The awe factor rises significantly to the event when you add a fifty-five minute cardiac arrest after nine days postop. More details about the cardiac arrest will come later. Thankfully my cardiac arrest did not occur after being discharged from the hospital, which was almost the case. If I had been discharged before the event occurred, I most likely would not be here today to write. At the very least, I would not have survived with all of the mental and physical abilities to write.

According to most medical publications, irreversible brain damage should occur after fifteen to twenty minutes without a heartbeat and oxygen deprivation. Thankfully, I am seeing and feeling more and more improvements with each passing day. My strength and stamina are returning to pre-diagnosis levels and I have gained enough weight to warrant a mild rebuke from my family doctor, Dr. Swan.

I have been experiencing this trial and error kind of relationship with food. In some ways, eating has become an adventure. I have a third less stomach, approximately ten inches less bowel, my gallbladder was removed, and about one third less pancreas. There are some foods that do not set well with me. I am painfully learning what those foods are but I will persevere. To simply overeat can now turn into an embarrassing episode. I believe one divine purpose in all of this was that God helped me to bring my appetite under control. If that is the case, it has certainly worked.

I do not fully understand the doctor's rebuke for my weight gain. After all, I started the year 2013 at a robust two hundred and ninety pounds. Ten months later, I weighed in at a measly two hundred and three pounds. I know the doctor has my best interest in mind. The potential for discontinuing an already reduced daily insulin dosage is a very real possibility. There is a possibility I will be able to discontinue the daily dose of blood thinner, and go back to an aspirin a day as it was before surgery. These and other things are a few of the many blessings I am realizing at this point in my recovery. I do covet the prayers of my Christian friends as I go forward. I have no doubt it is the prayers that have sustained me throughout this ordeal and continue through today.

As I close this segment and continue this work, I do so with a new and deeply engrained knowledge of the temporary nature of life, the certainty of death, and all the fear and fantasy that accompany it. I have had a taste of the peace, warmth, and security an eternity with Christ can hold. I could never describe the peace I felt during the time there was no breath in my body. I know the memory of that feeling will remain a source of security for the rest of my life. Though my prognosis is miraculously good,

I realize my body is still dying. I know that I as well as all the rest of us, will face the reality of death at some point in the future.

Death is inevitably as much a part of living as living is in itself. This is not a truth we should fear as a Christian because the sting of death has now been removed! Death is a transition and transformation! One year ago, I felt what could have been the very last breath leave my body. I could not find another one! The real question for you today is this…..do you know the one who holds your very next breath in His hands? I am so thankful that I do!!

I precede this article by sharing some thoughts I was inspired to pen during the Christmas season of 2012 in "The Long Journey Home". At the time I wrote these thoughts, I remember feeling very uneasy, having a troubled spirit. It was as though God was bringing me to a place where I could see and feel the temporary nature of this life, while showing me the beauty awaiting at the other end of it. I remember praying as I wrote and asking God if He was preparing me for death or for the death of someone I loved. His spirit continued to complete the message bringing clarity to what true "Home" should look like to a child of God.

Six months later, my prayer was answered. He was preparing me for death but not the death of my body…..God was only holding my breath for a while. He was preparing me for the death of my own independent will. He was helping me to see more clearly His divine will for me. At the time I wrote "The Long Journey Home," there was no cancer diagnosis, no pulmonary embolism, and no code blue. There was only God and His message was clear, "You are not home yet!"

I believe God's message for every Christian is this, to make the most of the life He has given us and to fulfill His purposes! God will never give up on the purpose He has appointed for you. Every life has a divine purpose. God will allow us to choose whether we fulfill it or not. Surrender to His purpose now!! I assure you, it will save you much pain and heartache later, either in this life or in the next. To live at odds with your Creator is not the place you want to be!! If you are truly a child of God, He will never lose sight of where you are or where you need to be! If you are not a believer, He will never quit trying to bring you back home. He will always know where to find you and how to get your attention…..and He will find you!

My Family, a Time to Rejoice and Give Thanks
Our First Thanksgiving Together after Our Miracle!

Article Three: Personal Message
from the Author

Since reading a book requires such a large investment of our precious time, I think people should have a good presentation about the author. This knowledge will help determine if the read is worthwhile for them. Most of us read because we want new insight or we want to glean the knowledge of the experiences from someone else. We read with the hope that the knowledge or insight of the author will help to open our own mind to new possibilities. We may sometimes read with the hope of finding help in dealing with certain real life situations that stare us in the face every waking hour of our day.

Certain authors we find very relatable, while others…..not so much. In the next few paragraphs and chapters, I'd like to introduce myself and some of the most important life lessons that I have learned during my own spiritual odyssey. These are the lessons that are motivating me to write. It is an effort to try to make a difference for all who may be seeking their own personal answers. It is my hope that you will choose to invest your time reading my reflections, stories, and opinions. I have gleaned many revelations that I believe will be a spiritually challenging, motivating, and rewarding experience for you. This is my sole purpose and reason for doing this work.

I grew up in a simple farm family in eastern Tennessee. Both of my parents were of Scots-Irish descent. We were not wealthy in a monetary sense but the things we did have were a blessing. The good work ethic and drive of my dad along with the maternal and Godly commitment of my mother was the glue holding it all together in those early days. Dads' family relocated from Sevierville Tennessee to a few acres in southern Bradley County. This property was near the Georgia line in a place the locals referred to as Buck's Pocket.

My grandfather was one of twelve children, birthed by the same mother. Not all twelve children had the same biological father. History seems to indicate their mother could have been a prostitute for the early years of her life. She eventually settled down with the man who would become my great-grandfather. My grandma Dunn was a feisty Scots Irish who came from a family acquainted with living hard and having experienced their fair share of hardships. She experienced her share of abuse from my grandfather in the early years. He had a tendency to drink too much and become violent in those early years of his life. Thankfully, later in life He met the one who brought peace to his troubled soul. His heart was softened for the rest of his days. We all loved him, however, I am not sure he was ever fully able to forgive himself.

My mother was born into a family of sharecroppers. She grew up very poor in North Georgia near the little town of Cohutta, south of Buck's Pocket. They made their living growing and harvesting cotton. She told us of how they would pick cotton until their fingers bled. They worked very hard to make ends meet. I never knew my granddad Williams. He had a hard life and died when my mother was very young. My granny Williams became one of the earliest spiritual influences in my life. She knew the scriptures well and she lived them to the best of her ability. She expected us to do the same if she had any say in the matter. And believe me, there were not many who could keep granny Williams from ever having her say.

She was always aware of what was going on around her. I remember many times when I would be arguing with my siblings and say something out of line only to find the back of granny Williams hand across my mouth. Even worse, she would drop down on me with the full force of her body and start praying down the angels on my head, driving the demons away. She believed in immediate discipline and she never hesitated to give it liberally. My mother inherited the same spiritual resolve and zeal. I did not know what a blessing this was at the time. I do now! This is exactly the kind of mothering the world needs today.

The rare occasion when my Grandparents were all together at another much earlier Thanksgiving celebration

Through the influence of my parents and grandparents, and eventually through those in our community, I came to a place where I had to make my own decisions about what to do with the Jesus I had been taught about all my life. One Sunday morning, at the ripe old age of nine, I made the decision to receive Jesus as my Savior. I became a child of God. I did not have a clue what it meant to be a child of God. I did not comprehend the meaning of "living a life of faith" and fully committed to pleasing God and not myself.

As I struggled to give God His rightful place of authority in my life, this and many other things would come much later. The experience of being saved left me with a certainty that whatever my sins were, and would ever be, had been forgiven. I knew whatever my life would ultimately become was under Gods control. It was He who had given my life in the first place. For the time it was enough.

As time clicked along, I learned many things from those who were my examples in the faith. I received many gifts from the saints I was blessed to know. Ronnie Hooker was one such saint. He was our choir director and encouraged us to use our talents for the Lord. He later answered his own call to pastor until his untimely heart attack and death at a very early age. One of my fondest memories of him occurred as I stood over my granny Williams' casket during her funeral. She was my first grandparent to answer the call to come home and I was learning to say my last farewell. I was having a hard time until I felt these huge, strong hands, take me around the shoulders and hold me up. It was Ronnie and I will never forget that day. I will never forget him.

And then there was our pastor, T.R. Ethridge who guided me through those first few years as a babe in Christ. He preached the message which brought conviction to my soul and led me to salvation. He is still with us today and is a cherished part of my spiritual memory bank. He recently came to hear me speak as I gave my testimony and shared the Word. I will never forget his sense of humor and the way he could bring calm to any storm. He was still giving encouragement after all these years. My other pastor, Marvin West, later helped to establish me in the ministry. He was a gifted leader in helping to establish us in ministry as we accepted our own calls to answer Gods plan for our lives. Marvin always referred to himself in the plural. Instead of "me", it was "us" or "we" when he referred to himself. I had asked him why he did that and he replied, "Because I am never alone.….Jesus and the Holy Spirit are always with me." I discovered not long after our conversation that I had begun to do the same thing. We are truly "never alone." We should never forget it. We recently said goodbye to Marvin. He left this world as a result of the injuries he sustained from a dozer accident on his farm.

And then there was Ms. Buckner, a lady who invested her whole life in teaching children the ways of God. For many years and well beyond childhood, I would receive her little hand-made cutouts and various written messages by mail. I am sure many other adult children in the community have experienced the same thing. Her messages always seemed to come at the most opportune times as though she knew my needs even though I had not told her. I had not seen her. Mrs. Buckner was one of my early angels. The mailings eventually stopped. She had answered her call to come home. Her work was done and those she impacted were eternally changed.

After all of these things and too many others to mention, I found myself in a place where I had to choose between the things I had been taught and the things I was learning from the world around me. There had come a time when the faith I had received, as a result of the influence of godly people around me, had to somehow become my own faith. God did not want me to love Him because others had told me I should love Him. He wanted me to love him because I recognized the abundant love He had bestowed upon me. He wanted me to love Him because of an intimate and holy bond He had made possible in Christ. I knew this was the only way I could find the abundant life He had in mind for me.

My relationship grew. God did not want me to serve Him out of a feeling of obligation or because others had shamed me into it. He wanted me to serve him so I would know a whole new level of divine fellowship. This is a fellowship that only comes when faith has been put into action. Finally, all my experiences lead me to the ministry of the Word. God did not want me to read His Word and glean only the things I had been taught by many well-meaning teachers and pastors. He wanted me to apply my faith to the Word, trust the spirit for interpretation, and to proclaim the truth regardless of what everyone else says or does. I had no idea of the pain and misery that would be involved in getting me to the place where I could be faithful to God's Word, and God alone. This is a work that continues even now, every day. I am not yet there.

I take up this work now because it is the foundation for the beginning of the rest of my life. This work is the action God is calling me to do today. I am compelled to be faithful to the calling. It comes because of the ways God has intervened in my life for the past fifty years. It comes as a result of the lessons I have learned as the beneficiary of a miraculous and supernatural moving of God in my personal life. This was a moving that I could have never expected. The result of this divine visitation has been both a physical and spiritual healing. A holistic and complete deliverance has been achieved.

Social Media- Legacy of Prayer and Faith:

Posted by: Beverly Rollins Dunn – August 26th, 2013
Moon Shadows Tn.

I am in the peacefulness of my hiding place, taking a few minutes to rest from the busy time of getting things together for tomorrow. "Be Still" keeps coming to me. It came yesterday, in the hymn by Steven Curtis Chapman and as the song played we were passing Macedonia Baptist Church and the same scripture was on their sign. I drew Tony's attention to both......and all I could say was "Thank You Sweet Father"...... I am finding myself more emotional today as the surgery time draws near. You take for granted the routine, everyday activities that are really great, like regular work, errands to run, meals together and family time. Then there are the special times together, as a couple and are really wonderful. When you see changes on the horizon, you feel really good about everyday normal. I believe there is a purpose in it all and I am trusting God about the changes in the routine, because I have the assurance that He loves me so much. Tomorrow morning, we have to be at the hospital at 6:30am. Tony is scheduled for the Whipple procedure, by Dr. Charles Portera, Jr. The surgery will be four to six hours and he will go straight from there to ICU for two to three days. Please pray for Tony, the doctor and nurses, and everyone else involved. Please pray for Tony to have peace, complete healing, and recovery beyond expectations. Please pray for Tony's mom and dad, the kids and grandkids as it is not an easy thing to be the onlooker. Pray for me to stay strong and be still, for as many may know, that is not one of my strong points. LOL. I do know He is God though. Pray through it all, that God will be glorified in everyone and everything.

Ps. 46:10 Be still, and know that I am God;.....NKJV

Only God is able to reveal the deepest cancers lurking within our bodies as well as those in our souls. Only God is able to orchestrate the events which lead to our deliverance from both. In my case it was pancreatic cancer, one of the most stealth and deadly enemies of the body. Adding insult to injury and even more emphasis of the divine deliverance was a pulmonary embolism that caused cardiac arrest. It stopped my heart for a period of fifty-five minutes in my recovery process.

This event left all of those who shared and witnessed it in absolute amazement. What they witnessed take place with me, and my ultimate survival, is considered a medical impossibility.....a "miracle!" What I have realized as a result of their testimonies is that they became un-expecting eye-witnesses to an undeniable fact. It is God who holds life and deliverance in His hands. For many, this event caused a paradigm shift in both their natural and spiritual understanding and thinking. It has left an indelible mark in their minds and on their lives.

It is this experience which brings the thoughts of mighty angel wings and deliverance into my perspective. Those involved in my ordeal, September 6, 2013, had no idea that their typical day as a medical professional at Memorial hospital would burn something into their memories that they would never forget. They were drawn into something far bigger than medical science on that day. The surreal power of God would rest upon each one of them as their hands and their feet became divine instruments to accomplish His purpose.

According to many of the accounts I have been given, there was an unseen yet undeniable presence in the treatment rooms, the hallways and corridors, the waiting rooms, and even stairwells that day. The angels gathered that day and they accomplished the thing they were created to accomplish. They glorified God!! They did it through those who were willing to loan them their hands and feet as well as their hearts.

Social Media-Legacy of Prayer and Faith:

Posted by: Beverly Rollins Dunn – August 27th, 2013
Moon Shadows Tn.

So, Tony had a total surgery time of 5.5 hours. Talked with Dr. Portera and he says everything went well. Tentative specimens are negative for cancer. We have not seen him but we are told that he looks really good for all that was done. We have had visitors to stop in to pray with us and we so appreciate that. Thanks Dewayne Pierce, Don and Nancy Fenton, and Todd Colbert.

Ex 14:14 The Lord will fight for you and you shall hold your peace…..NKJV

Since being released from the hospital, and after a lengthy time of refreshing and regaining of strength, I have resumed life as before. I have returned to my job of almost forty years as a battery maker. As a result of the powerful drugs and the trauma I experienced, I have noticed a little loss of concentration and a few memory issues. I feel very "normal" again. In fact, my wife Bev and I took a delayed 20th wedding anniversary trip to Europe. Our trip was one year after starting my new life, 2014. This was our 21st wedding anniversary, celebrating our 20th anniversary that I slept through. Bev refers to it as our 20th anniversary with one to grow old on. Quite fitting I might add!

I have undertaken many home improvement projects. Bev and I are preparing for a wedding at our home as our son Derrick ties the knot. Even today, I completed my third round of golf since I was released from the hospital almost two years ago. Of course, in the midst of all this activity, I write! I sometimes wonder if I will ever finish this written work. I then remember that God has gone to great lengths to give me the opportunity to live this life I live and to give Him glory for it. I will not disappoint Him.

As a minister, it is fitting that I can now look back at all the ways in which I have been deceived about my role in accomplishing God's will and pleasing Him. I have held numerous church related positions including pastor, music director, teacher, bus driver, and many other roles. I have studied and preached for over thirty years. I have done all this in an effort to please and be used by God. I realize that in the moment of my greatest weakness, when I was unable to speak or to respond, He accomplished more than I ever could have with my human efforts. Through His marvelous works, He touched the lives of my family, my friends, and my medical angels in ways I never could.

Strangely enough, my only role in this great moving event took place many years earlier when I made a commitment to Him. I made Him a promise that I was willing to do whatever it would take to accomplish His purpose. I placed my life, with all of my imperfections, completely in His hands. This is the greatest and wisest decision I have ever made. I believe it is the sole reason I am still here today. He remembers our commitments and He is not finished with me. I have heard this message repeatedly from nurses, doctors, family, friends, and the many other hospital employees who were witness our special event.

As I live each day anew, there is not a time when this special visitation eludes my memory. There is no forgetting the special purpose of it all— for my angels will not let me. As I have returned to visit the medical staff and as I converse with coworkers who shared this special time with us, there is one message that continues to reoccur in our conversations. The message.....“God’s not through with you yet!” I feel the presence of God every time I walk the hallways of Memorial Hospital and every time I look into the smiling faces of those who cared for us. Whose angels are they today, I wonder? They will always be mine!

This is a book about deliverance, faith, being obedient, and then seeing the salvation of an Almighty and Holy God. It is about the journey that faith takes us on once we commit to it. This book is about how we choose to respond and relate to the presence of God on a daily basis. What a privilege He has given us and what blessings He has made us partakers of!! If you choose to read, it is my hope that you will find new breath from heaven and will be drawn to a more intimate and interactive relationship with the Father, through His Son Jesus. May God grant you the kind of life that will be an example of power and praise to the world around you!

Article Four: Freedom to Choose

I was once asked by a Bible student why I thought God had placed the tree of the "Knowledge of Good and Evil" in the Garden of Eden. Would it not have been much safer to leave it out, to prevent the possibility that humanity would be disobedient? I thought his question was excellent. It caused me to spend a significant amount of time in study and meditation. He was right. It would have been much simpler if God had put safeguards into place to prevent us from making a spiritually fatal mistake. After all,

He is God, He created everything, and He knows what is best for us! This is most certainly a true statement.

I believe the answer to the question is one which reveals a tremendous amount of knowledge and understanding about the character and personality of God. I believe the real answer has to do with the fact that God has no reason or need to attach himself to the human creature. He is very secure being God. He *needs* nothing! As a result of His love for humanity, He desires a meaningful relationship with us. Albeit, He does not desire a relationship so badly He will force us into it. He deliberately designed it to be our choice, our responsibility. The verbal picture presented in Genesis places the Tree of the Knowledge of Good and Evil in the same proximity in the Garden with that of another special tree, The Tree of Life. These trees were diametrically opposed to one another, one representing eternal life while the other represented eternal death. As it is now the stage for choice is set…..thanks to Jesus. On the cross, He became the new Tree of Life. The choice is once again before us!

Without threat or intimidation on His part, He wants us to choose Him willingly. I believe this is why we find the tree in the garden. The lesser god Allah, with his extremist hit-men, is making headlines more often today. Allah never has and never would afford humanity such freedom. Instead, his allure is one of fear and death. Interpretation of his doctrine, by many, makes him a tyrant. He becomes a blood thirsty murderer forcing his will on humanity. I have often questioned how many adherents his religion would have if not for the fear and threat of death hanging over their heads. There is no other doctrine comparable to that of the just and gracious, soon coming judge, God of the Bible. It is my position that all others are counterfeits which allure humanity away from the truth.

Choice is a powerful thing! We spend every day of our lives making choices. Many times we make our choices without giving a second thought of how those choices will impact our lives and the lives of those we love. At some point in our lives, when we have grown old enough and hopefully wise enough, we can look back over both tragedies and triumphs to see the truth. Our choices are the seeds which ultimately determine and shaped who we become. The results of those choices grow and blossom and are producing fruit in our lives and in some cases those choices are the cause for a lack of fruit. Many of us have not been wise in our choices of the seed we chose to plant or in how we chose to plant them. We are amazed at how small and insignificant we thought those choices were at the time. How wrong we were!

Although this option to choose carries with it a great responsibility, it is ultimately this option that proves our worthiness for the coming kingdom of God. If we choose to reject God, we reject every effort of love He has shown us through the years. Many times we say to Him, "No Thanks, I'd prefer to go it alone. I choose to not believe your truths." In making this choice, we will seal our spiritual and eternal doom. It breaks the heart of God but He will not force us to change our mind. It is our decision. We will live with it and we will ultimately die with it.

But there is another choice! This choice is one of embracing God as our Creator, as our provider, and as the one who brings about abundant life for all who call upon Him. He promises us if we choose to acknowledge Him in all our ways, then He will direct our paths (Prov. 3:6). He leads us through those dangerous places where many often crash and burn. It means He lovingly takes us through those times that we would never have chosen for ourselves. It will produce in us a more superior strength and spirit.

Even when we choose to acknowledge and serve God, there is a warning that we should heed. When we commit ourselves to Him, we are giving up our freedom to make the haphazard choices that become so natural. Instead, we choose to replace them with the challenges and blessings of seeking His will. Seeking first the kingdom of God (Matt. 6:33).

Life can now be experienced in a whole new light. I have chosen to let Him choose what is best for me. I am finding the answers to the many things that were mysteries before. I have given up on the flawed belief that I know what is best for myself and others. I willfully return to a place that I should have been all along. I can still see the tree in the garden. It is ever before me. I have access to eat of this tree it at any time…..but it is my choice not to eat.

Social Media-Legacy of Prayer and Faith:

**Posted by: Beverly Rollins Dunn – August 27th, 2013
Chattanooga Tn.**

Praises!!! Justin and I just visited Tony, in MICU and
unbelievable.....he is awake, color is great, eating ice,
talking, a little uncomfortable but no great pain. He said
they all find it hard to believe he is this well after that
surgery. Vital signs are great.....miracle! Thank you God
and all those praying to the Father on his behalf. Thank
you Kilee, Adelayde, and Elianna. Avi says he wants to see
you guys.

**Ps. 73:26 My flesh and my heart fail; But God is the
strength of my heart and my portion forever …..NKJV**

The table God has prepared for me is far better. If I ever make a
choice that is contrary to His plan and His purpose for my life, I choose
and desire for Him to intervene on my behalf. I take great joy in knowing
He is faithful to do that. I have given Him permission. This is the most
important choice I have ever made! I have no doubt this is why He has
been there in the trying times of my life and specifically in the hospital
room that day in September.

Article Five: Choices That Lead
to Divine Intervention

In recounting the many divine interventions that my family and I
encountered during his ordeal, I would like to share significant past
decisions and events that I believe set these current experiences into
motion. These decisions have left us in awe of the power and majesty of
the God we serve. I must begin with a very important decision I made in
October of 2010. This decision came about after a long struggle and much
prayer concerning the truths that God had been revealing to me during
my adult Christian life. These things are related to my personal Christian
walk and my role in the operation and formalities of the church.

I finally accepted what God was saying to me and I yielded. I made a decision to begin living my life devoid of the religious formalisms that I call "churchianity." This religious formalism had trapped me. I had allowed it to become a barrier in my relationship to God. Please allow me to explain…..the formality of church cannot substitute for a relationship with God. I believe God was pleased with my courage to hear Him and to step outside of what had become my comfort zone. My main issue, and I believe God's main issue, is with the direction the church is being led. The body has been divided into little pieces by its leaders and has been weakened. It seems we are more interested in our own particular flavor of Jesus than we are in unity and truth. Many of you know what I mean because you see and struggle with the same thing. You may not realize it now or you may not be able to muster the courage to admit it.

I did not abandon my affiliation and relationship with the people of God. The most precious and powerful times we have on this earth are when we spend time with blood kin, especially those who share a common bond through the blood of Christ. With all of our imperfections, we are all in this thing together. Our greatest need is to realize that He mostly uses "plain folk." "……from babes and nursing infants, He can perfect praise. (Mat 21:16 NKJV)"

We are all imperfect creatures seeking to grow to perfection through the Holy Spirit and the Word. The problem…..we have lost sight of the purpose and the objectives of the church and most certainly what our individual role should be. We have been convinced that we should leave the running of the church to "the professionals" and in many cases these professionals abuse the trust of the people. More importantly, they abuse trust of God.

As a result, we have allowed these hallowed offices to become perverted from that which was originally ordained. The motives for this perversion are simple. Many pastors, and other church leaders, have duped a scripturally seeking and spiritually immature body of believers. For personal gain, they desire to attain positions of authority where they can control and manipulate the people of God. This is the very thing Jesus rebuked the temple leaders for doing. This condition exists today, in epidemic proportions in our churches and in the airwaves and media.

Church is about much more than padded pews, printed programs, choirs, sermons, tithes and gifts, and other formalities in which we have become accustomed. To many times we have been enslaved by these things. These are the things I have been inspired to warn other fellow believers about. I have grown to realize it is this religious formalism that is transforming us into a powerless and worldly institution. We are imploding upon ourselves instead of exploding onto the world as was the case in the beginning. I shiver when I think about the many deceived church members participating in the church today. I fear they will face Christ one of these days only to hear those dreaded words, "Depart from me, ye that work iniquity."(Mat. 7:22-23 King James Version)

This is truly a time when we should be seeking a genuine and powerful relationship with Christ instead of the empty and powerless compromise of church membership. Church membership is simply not enough for a legitimate child of God. Sitting on a church pew every Sunday will not make one a Christian any more than standing in a circus rink will make one an elephant.

It is a great price to pay to fit into the format rather than walk a simple walk of obedience in the power of the spirit. God can accomplish more in one spirit filled believer than He can through ten thousand religious men pleasers. Our pastors and professional church leaders will bear a great burden of judgment when God finally comes to judge His church. I believe many have unintentionally led us to become exactly what the apostle Paul prophesied, by the Holy Spirit, in the New Testament. However, some have been very intentional in their deception. Paul warned us that we would have a form of Godliness, but deny His power (2 Tim.3:5). The key word here is "form". Believe me, we Christians are the masters of "form and formality." Everyone seems to have their own special "way" or "ways" of getting to God!

As Christians, we must be keenly attuned to the fact that God has gone to great lengths to keep us from developing "forms." These forms can become substitutes for His power and presence in our lives. In these modern days, we have become guilty of religious idolatry in the way we have chosen to approach a Holy God. Throughout the Holy Bible, there is a reason God has taken such care to warn His children about making forms and graven images. He understands our tendencies to be manipulated and controlled by what we see and by what we build. This is why the prohibition against idols is specifically mentioned in the Ten Commandments (Ex. 20: 4).

In many cases, we are more concerned about the size of the church building and the furnishings rather than what transpires in the church while we are assembled there. I know of instances where churches have split simply because they could not agree on what color the new carpet should be. Am I wrong or have our priorities gotten terribly out of sorts? I have searched and searched but could not find any reference in the scripture for the color of the carpet, the sound of the music or choir, not even the eloquence of the preacher (except to warn us about "enticing words"). Today, we are experiencing carnal Christian living at its best, or worst….. unfortunately. It seems to be the predominant rule and very rarely the exception.

For the most part, worship has been reduced to religious entertainment as we listen to the choir, a special singer, or "praise team". We then listen to a message from the preacher and go home feeling good about ourselves. If we do feel convicted, it is not because of our personal sin and our failure to please God. It is because we hear from the pulpit how we are not doing enough to support the programs or "forms" of the institution. This is an extremely dangerous condition and most members of the church today seem absolutely oblivious to it.

In large part, this ignorance is due to the collective efforts of many church leaders. They indoctrinate us into believing the real work of the church must be left to them. I am afraid many of our church leaders today are much more interested in taking care of themselves in order that they may be served by the church. Many are more interested in job security and less interested in eternal security, their service to Christ, the church, and the children of God.

I am afraid in far too many scenarios they have become the wolves in sheep's clothing as the scripture warned us. The scriptures describe this scenario best, "For such are false apostles, deceitful workers, transforming themselves into apostles of Christ. 14 And no wonder! For Satan transforms himself into an angel of light."(2 Cor. 11:13-14 New King James Version) In this perilous age we are in, it behooves us to pray for discernment that we may recognize the imposters! They are many! They are leading the church down a "broad way", on a pathway ending in destruction.

In His rebuke of the scribes and Pharisee's of His day Jesus set the perfect example in recognizing this sort of religious formality. I am convinced that He is beginning to do the same with what the church is becoming in this modern age. This formalism is the very reason the Christian church is in such a decline, numerically and influentially speaking. It is one of the reasons hatred from the world has reached epidemic proportions. Our hypocrisy infuriates them! But I digress, I have come to the point where I can fully accept these ugly truths about deceptions in my own life. This has set the table for the divine encounter about which I write.

This encounter has permanently and eternally changed my perspective on my God and His purpose for my life. God is more than willing to reveal His power to those who are willing to simply respond to His voice. God will reveal His power to those who surrender to Him alone. When we become willing to forsake and reject all the idols in our lives, including those of the religious variety, we will find God's voice can be very clearly discerned.

Social Media-Legacy of Prayer and Faith:

Posted by: Beverly Rollins Dunn – August 28th, 2013 Chattanooga Tn.

Major update with Tony, he was moved from MICU to a regular room because he was doing so well. The staff of Dr. Portera and Memorial Hospital have been great. Big thank you to friend, Barbara Dickerson and her nurse pals in preop and OR. Medical professionals that hear Tony has to have the Whipple procedure, always have a bad look and either say oh no or the like. After the Whipple, they are just amazed and can't believe his progress. His nurse that received him last night stated "I am not meaning to be fresh with your husband, but he is the best looking Whipple patient I have seen." When he was transferred to the floor earlier one of the receiving nurses said " So he had the Whipple Monday?" To which the MICU nurse replied, "No, just yesterday." His MICU nurse today has been a big golf fan like Tony and they have discussed not only golf statistics but Tony explained to him that golf was how this problem was first noticed so, the joke among the MICU guys and Tony is that golf saved his life.....lol.....I suggested that maybe Tony could get in on the PGA Tour for advertisement and his response was, "that is the only way I will get on the PGA tour." Please continue to pray for his recovery and please say a special prayer for the sweet family who adopted me in the ICU waiting area last night. They had me bring my chair to their area for security and comfort. I slept well. Thank you also to Todd and Danielle Collins for the visit and note last night. White Oak is blessed to have you guys. Thank you, David and Angela Coffey, for visiting today with me. Thanks to all of our family and friends for your wonderful love and support. It just means so much, praising God for all things.

I recently attended a service at my home church. It was my first speaking engagement after being released from the hospital. When I say home church, I am speaking of the place where I first came to a saving knowledge of Jesus Christ and was born again. It doesn't matter how old a person gets they will never forget the place where they first met Jesus. It will always be a special place. Although it has been over forty years since I attended there as a member, it was certainly a blessing to go back. God opened the door for me to share my testimony of His amazing power in our deliverance and healing.....an invitation I anxiously accepted.

After the service that day, God chose to bless me in a very special way. God really understood I was trying, with all my might, to understand exactly what was happening in our healing experience. More importantly, why was it happening? My answer began to become clear when the young pastor, a man I had attended church with when he was a young boy, mentioned a sermon that he had heard me preach many years ago. He looked at me with a confident eye and he asked me a question. "Do you remember a sermon you preached one time on Divine Appointments? Well, I have never forgotten that sermon. It has stuck with me ever since."

I am pretty sure the wisdom of God was shining through this young pastor. At this moment, I started getting the answer I was looking for! Of the many things I have forgotten through the years, that particular sermon was not one of them. I think it had as profound an effect upon my life as it did his—I needed a little memory jog. Thank you pastor Larry, God used you that moment.

Divine appointments! The entirety of the lives of all true believers, and the community of humanity in general, is comprised of a series of divine appointments! I say this on the authority of God's Holy Word. As believers, we fail to understand the significance of the scripture that declares, "For you were bought at a price;" (1 Cor. 6:20 NKJV). You are not your own person anymore! This is a description of what every believer should understand about their relationship with God. We have given up control of every aspect of our lives to allow the perfect divine will of God to reign. And yes, I understand the difficulty of actually being able to completely submit.

Sometimes in ignorance, and in pure defiance at others, I have been trying to call the shots in my life based on my own will. I have not submitted to my heavenly Father as I should have. For much of my Christian, life I have lived in rebellion. The above scripture reference is a warning to all believers. Every decision and every desire that we may ever have must first come under the scrutiny and authority of the Holy Spirit. No task or action, no message, no outreach of any kind should be undertaken unless it is first ordained in heaven.

It is hard for any person to give up their natural identity in order to allow Christ to develop a new identity for them. Fortunately, the entire Christian experience is absolutely contingent on our willingness to do that. Yes, it is true that God loves me just as I am. But, He has absolutely zero desire to leave me that way. I am thankful that God feels this way. The unbelieving world cannot fathom this principle. The divine purpose in all that God has done to reveal Himself to the world centers around the fact that as sinners we are powerless to change our own tainted nature.

Social Media-Legacy of Prayer and Faith:

Posted by: Beverly Rollins Dunn – August 30th, 2013 Chattanooga Tn.

Update on Tony. He is still progressing at an amazing pace. He has one IV line remaining, the two drains, and his stomach tube, of which he is now receiving feedings. As the nurse was connecting the feeding, Tony voiced his concern for his body's response to it and we mentioned we would pray that it went well. She finished her task and states, "I will be glad to pray with you about the feeding." We prayed together. What blessings of God's love and placement of precious people in our path. Tony is walking and drains continue to show no leak from the surgery connections. We ask that you continue to pray that complete and solid healing takes place, that the feeding goes well, and general recovery continues.

Every gift that God has given us removes our excuses. It is through those gifts that God can change us. He can transform us into a new and beautiful creation. Only He can change the unholy to the holy and the unrighteous to the righteous. He not only wants us to surrender to our own sinful nature, He wants us to *submit* our sinful nature "to Him." He can take it from there. Deep down, this is the true deliverance we all know we need and desire so badly. If we refuse to allow Christ to remake us after His image, for whatever reason, He can never be glorified in us! We will be living in rebellion. This rebellion is either a misunderstanding and happens ignorantly because we have ignored His Word, or because we have not sincerely sought after the intimate relationship God desires to have with us. It can happen as a result of our willful disobedience. In my case, it happened because I chose to believe that God would not use me. As an imperfect and broken man, I doubted that he would accomplish His revealed purposes in my life and in the world around me.

I knew what He wanted of me but I did not feel worthy to perform it. I chose to look at the religious establishment that I had found myself a part of and I had yielded to its authority rather than to His. Indeed, there are many professing believers who have wanted Jesus as their Savior. However, the profession is in order to avoid hell and condemnation while denying Him Lordship over their lives. They did not allow God to make them new. They did not follow Him to the destination He had chosen for them.

Many have chosen to hide underneath an umbrella of religious formality and service. They live out their spiritual lives vicariously through the professionals they hire. In other words, we have paid the preacher to do many of the things God called us to do. This is the overarching spiritual sin of most well-meaning Christians. This condition guarantees that there will be a divine appointment in our future. God will never be satisfied until He is Lord of your life and He alone!! He will never be satisfied with a child who merely practices a form of religion but does not seek an active and intimate relationship with Him.

I want to remind you of another scripture now burning in my mind. The scripture reads something like this, " 6 For whom the LORD loves He chastens, and scourges every son whom He receives. 7 If you endure chastening, God deals with you as with sons; for what son is there whom a father does not chasten? 8 But if you are without chastening, of which all have become partakers, then you are illegitimate and not sons." (Heb.12:6—8 NKJV) If you feel you are a believer, but have not felt the divine and powerful hand of God guiding you to His chosen destination, it may be time for a check-up. Make sure you are totally yielded and available to God's will.

Social Media- Legacy of Prayer and Faith:

Posted by: Beverly Rollins Dunn – September 2, 2013 Chattanooga Tn.

Tony's progression update ☺. He is still making an awesome recovery. He is walking more, with a little encouragement.....LOL.....and he is now on a full liquid diet. All systems are a go and the digestive system seems to be awake. I could talk about this stuff all day long but I will spare you my FB family and friends all the details and just address on part by saying, I never thought certain sounds would fall under the term "joyful noise".....haha. Please continue in prayer for his diet and gaining in digestive function. We have been having a little trouble with his stomach tube becoming clogged, causing minor issues. Thank you all, praises and thanksgiving to our Father.

Rom. 12:12 …..rejoicing in hope, patient in tribulation, continuing steadfastly in prayer;…..NKJV

What has God taught me throughout these past few months of one miracle, one divine intervention after another? He has taught me how wonderful it is to be loved by a wife and children, parents, brothers and sisters, and in-laws who spent many sleepless nights not knowing but never giving up. He has taught me how precious it is to have friends who are willing to interrupt their busy schedules to pray and visit and to show how much they care. These friends do the most kind and helpful things to help alleviate at least some of the stress and pain. He has helped me to see the beautiful nature of many in the health care profession, especially those who are there because they have a genuine passion for people. These are people who are willing to work themselves to near exhaustion in order to save your life. I am so thankful they did!

He has proven to me that death is not to be feared for those who are truly His child. He has taught me that He has the same life giving power today, as He had on the day He breathed life into a motionless Adam. He has shown me that He can intervene in the life of man in a way that leaves the man, the doctors, the nurses, and his own family in awe. They witnessed God's work. For His work far exceeded and trumped all medical boundaries and expectations. He has shown me that He understands my doubts and feelings of inferiority. God injected Himself into my life in such a way that it leaves me feeling as though I could have been the only man on earth. He has shown me there is nothing in the earth that His people should fear. He is able to subdue and hold all our enemies at bay including, the greatest of all enemies, death! Why should I ever fear people when I serve such an all- powerful God? By God's grace and power, I will never fear again!

Social Media-Legacy of Prayer and Faith:

Posted by: Beverly Rollins Dunn – Sept. 3rd, 2013 Chattanooga Tn.

We have had a big day and a blessed day. The Dr. was by to check on Tony and continues to be thrilled with his progress. We are possibly going home in two days and possibly without his tubes. He also had the final pathology report that had shown a couple of spots, in the pancreatic cysts, of invasive cancer cells but the nodes are clear and the surgery took care of it. We feel so grateful and blessed. Praise God for it all! Thank you all for praying.

Phil. 4:6 Be anxious for nothing, but in everything by prayer and supplication, with thanksgiving, let your request be made known unto God; 7 and the peace of God, which surpasses all understanding, will guard your hearts and minds through Christ Jesus…..NKJV

What is it God desires of me now? There is a reason that God has chosen to reveal Himself in such an awesome and powerful way! It may sound strange but God's desire for my life is the same as it has always been. He has realigned my priorities. It can be summed up in one word, LOVE! He wants me to love my family in such a way that His love is reflected into their lives. He wants me to love my friends and acquaintances He has brought into my life. He wants me to love those who really do not care for me, loving them to the point of making them angry if necessary. He wants me to love the truth to the point I will never compromise it. Instead, to be willing to take a jealous stand upon the truth even if it offends the whole world, as it most likely will. He wants me to make sure the relationship I share with Him is one based on a true love for His will and a pure faith on my part. This is a love that will guide me to place all my trust and hope in Him and in nothing or no one else.

He wants me to write and share the things He is showing me. There are many seeking to grow just as I am. God wants me to teach those who are teachable and rebuke those who are not, all of course in His Holy and Jealous Love! He wants me to stand toe to toe with demons, regardless of where they are or within whom they may be hiding. He wants me to let others know there is great healing in His mighty wings. God is Master and Lord of all!! This is still "His" world and in time God will come to judge and reclaim it. In our religious circles, this is a truth we have all lost sight of.

In short, He wants me to move from being a disciple of His word (hearer or learner) to being an apostle of His Word (applying His Truth and doing His Truth). The church today is full of hearers who are afraid, or do not know exactly how to apply what they have learned in a way that produces Holy action. When we apply and act on what God is teaching, we realize it will produce the same negative responses and retaliations from our world it did for the first apostles.

Today, the greatest need is for Christians is to come to a place where we begin to "Live Out" the truth of God. We must live this way in order to find the "personal cross" God has appointed for us. This is the plight many modern Christians are seeking desperately to avoid. Instead, we seek the smooth road, a road in which a crucified Christ is unfamiliar. It is a road the Holy Apostles were unfamiliar with as they all faced martyrdom or tribulation because of their faith. This is the road many other believers have refused to travel, choosing instead to "Please men, rather than God." Please hear me child of God.....God has not prepared a smooth road for you! The road He has prepared for you has no alternative routes and only you can travel it. He will not be fully satisfied with your life until you accept the road and the destination He has chosen for you. This is the greatest lesson He has taught me. And remember, the servant can never be greater than his lord. Hear now as Jesus proclaims to you, (Mark 10:21 NKJV) Then Jesus, looking at him, loved him, and said to him, "One thing you lack: Go your way, sell whatever you have and give to the poor, and you will have treasure in heaven; and come, take up the cross, and follow Me." This is the will of God! No alternatives! No substitutes! "He who has an ear, let him hear......" (Rev. 2:7 NKJV)

Social Media-Legacy of Prayer and Faith:

Posted by: Beverly Rollins Dunn – Sept. 5th, 2013 Chattanooga Tn.

Great day after a difficult evening. The G and J tubes have been a little problematic for us the past few days. Yesterday, Tony vomited for the first time. What we thought might be a set-back seems to have actually have been a reset and not pleasant in doing so. Tubes are functioning very well and Tony feels amazing today. Thank you to our caring and mighty God for the reset. My mind travels to other possible lessons we could learn from a loving Father and a reset button. ☺ We are requesting prayer for home and continued recovery there.

Isa. 61:3 To console those who mourn in Zion, To give them beauty for ashes, the oil of joy for mourning, the garment of praise for the spirit of heaviness; That they may be called trees of righteousness, the planting of the Lord, that He may be glorified.....NKJV

Chapter One

Miracle One, The Messenger on the Golf Course

From Golf Round to Ultrasound

"That day marked a paradigm shift in my thinking about life and death. I did not know it at the time but I would never think about death the same again. For now, things were dark, scary, and uncertain, but we had our hope and trust in the Lord. He was truly able to bring calm to our storm."

When God Comes Near

I am not sure we really understand this thing we call Christianity. We gather in our church houses and we participate in the activities surrounding our religion. For many of us, the activities we undertake are the culmination of our inner most desire to please our God and to show Him our adoration. But if pleasing Him is really our truest desire, we must allow the Spirit to bring us to the place where we can see the surrounding world through His eyes and feel it through the desire of His heart.

This end should be the objective of all our pursuits as believers. All of our efforts and activities should focus on achieving His pleasure and not our own. This means God receives all of our time. It is truly not our time at all, but His! Two or three hours every Sunday for our offering of praise and Thanksgiving is not enough. God should get twenty-four hours of every day.

I fully understand the difficulties of this truth and I have failed miserably through the years at living in such a way myself. It does not change the truth of the fact. It has always been so! As believers, we understand God is not restricted or motivated by any time table or schedule. Instead, He acts according to His divine will and is motivated by the needs of the moment. It can mean sending a deluge on the earth to judge wickedness, bringing about correction. It can mean sending a mighty wind to divide the waters of the Red Sea for God's chosen people to cross to their deliverance, while simultaneously destroying those who seek to destroy them. To the other extreme, God can visit His messenger hidden away in a cave, fearing for his life, and instruct him with a still small voice. God can deliver His servant who is held in a prison cell. The servant sees his chains fall off and the prison doors fling open. Certainly, God has proven over and over again that He has the authority to move nations or individuals with equal power and effect.

Knowing these things, for many years of my life, without actually expecting to see them in reality has been one of my gravest sins. How is it I could be so "faithfully unfaithful" to the majesty and power of the one I claim allegiance to? How can I love the God of Israel? He is the Father of all who live. He is the father of the Savior, Jesus Christ who brought full and complete deliverance to all who would receive it. How can I be so unfaithful to Him? All I can say, His patience and long- suffering toward His children is so powerfully amazing.

I am thankful He does not judge us by our failures through the passage of time but rather by what He sees in us as he looks into the future. He does not judge us by what we are now but by what He knows we will become. He knows those who will eventually rise in spiritual nobility and accept the mantle He has chosen for them. He looks forward to that time for all of us. It should not be a surprise to us if He shows up on the doorstep of our life with a clear and powerful message. If we have refused to listen to the still small voice that He has placed within all who believe, He knows how to get our attention.

Yes indeed, God cares so much to fulfill His truth in the world that He will visit each of those who will play a part in accomplishing it and in a close and personal way. With His visitation will come an uncommon power that cannot be adequately explained! It is for accomplishing a heavenly purpose in the earth. I am sure the last question of the mighty Pharaoh was how could these miracles possibly be? Or Goliath's last thought, how could this runt possibly defeat me? The answer, Pharaoh was not defeated by Moses. He was defeated by God, in Moses. Goliath was not defeated by David. He was defeated by God, in David. All of our victories will come the same way if we allow them to come at all!

In our world today, we have been witness to incomprehensible evils inflicted by tyrannical governments on their people, or cowardly terrorists in service to their self-imposed tyrannical god. In our own Christian society, we have seen a perversion of justice that leaves the innocent as victims of unspeakable evils, seemingly without a voice for their defense, while evildoers are rewarded. We have seen those who love their God, deep in their hearts, silenced and threatened. But never have we lived in such a time when the salvation of God is so near. His power has not waned! God's justice has not been revoked from heaven! He is still visiting His children who truly believe He will have the last word. And make no mistake about it, God will have the last Word!! We should take heart in this scripture, "And let us not grow weary while doing good for in due season we shall reap if we do not lose heart" (Gal 6:9 NKJV). The clouds may hide the light briefly and the world may seem hopelessly lost but it is only a matter of time until we will see His salvation. God is never too far away from those who love and seek Him. Do not give up on Him for He will certainly never give up on you. When you find you need Him the most, and maybe not in a way you would expect, He will show up!

Social Media-Legacy of Prayer and Faith:

Posted by: Suzanne Carson Bynum – Sept 6th, 2013

As we close our eyes tonight, please pray diligently for Tony Dunn, Beverly Rollins Dunn, and Family. Specifically requesting that he doesn't have bleeding complications in his brain or at the surgery site while receiving "clot busting" meds after being revived after 30 minutes of a hospital code. He is ventilated but responds well with hands and eyebrows to loved ones.....thanks prayer warriors.

As I share some of the stories of the events that occurred this past year, I hope to use the scriptures to help explain what I believe highlights the spiritual significance of these events. As a child of God, I have found that all of the scriptures are immensely powerful in helping us to understand the events and happenings of life. I love the scripture in Ecclesiastes where Solomon in his wisdom declares, ".....there is nothing new under the sun!" (Eccl. 1:9 NKJV) When it comes to the affairs of people, this is certainly true. Regardless of how long ago it may have been, the message in the scripture is a timeless one. The nature of humanity is the same now as it was when the Spirit first inspired the message. I have chosen the following passages to help begin the process of explaining what God has been saying to me concerning the way He has chosen to work in our lives and bring about these many miracles, or interventions.

Job Faces His Foe

(Job 2:3—7 NKJV) Then the LORD said to Satan, "Have you considered My servant Job, that there is none like him on the earth, a blameless and upright man, one who fears God and shuns evil? And still he holds fast to his integrity, although you incited Me against him, to destroy him without cause." 4 So Satan answered the LORD and said, "Skin for skin! Yes, all that a man has he will give for his life.5 But stretch out Your hand now, and touch his bone and his flesh, and he will surely curse You to Your face!"6 And the LORD said to Satan, "Behold, he is in your hand, but spare his life." 7 So Satan went out from the presence of the LORD, and struck Job with painful boils from the sole of his foot to the crown of his head.

The Apostle Paul Accepts His Plight

(2 Corinthians 12:7—10 NKJV) 7 "And lest I should be exalted above measure by the abundance of the revelations, a thorn in the flesh was given to me, a messenger of Satan to buffet me, lest I be exalted above measure. 8 Concerning this thing I pleaded with the Lord three times that it might depart from me. 9 And He said to me, "My grace

is sufficient for you, for My strength is made perfect in weakness." Therefore most gladly I will rather boast in my infirmities, that the power of Christ may rest upon me. 10 Therefore I take pleasure in infirmities, in reproaches, in needs, in persecutions, in distresses, for Christ's sake. For when I am weak, then I am strong.

God is so attuned to our daily lives and that He can choose to take the small things we love, such as the sport of golf, and interject Himself in a way to totally redirect our lives. In my experience, He has chosen to do that very thing. The story of my encounter and resulting healing (both spiritually and physically) began on a small nine-hole golf course in Destin, Florida, in the month of June, 2013. This was a round of golf that will always be special to me.....I will never forget it! Unfortunately, this is not because I played so well. It was because I came directly under the powerful hand of God in a way I had never expected or experienced.

The opening scriptures of this chapter are the two examples I think are most appropriate for the introduction to our story. I do not consider myself in the same league with such men of integrity and spiritual power as Job or the Apostle Paul. I truly do not. But rather, there are aspects in the story of each of these individuals that parallel some of the spiritual lessons God has taught me as we have traveled through each day of this experience.

In Jobs case, God used Satan to test the spiritual resolve of Job to a point that would have broken most people. The willingness of God to turn Satan loose, with limitations of course, on a human being to test his faith is a mystery that stupefies most of us. Yet it was necessary to provide Job, and us, the opportunity to see the victory that can come through simple but resolute faith. Not to mention, God would show Satan the benefits of staying true to the Almighty God. Satan would learn this lesson from God's man Job, a weak and feeble human being. The fact that God can use a "human" to defeat Satan, originally the second most powerful angel God ever created, is the ultimate insult to Satan.

In the Apostle Paul's case, no one knows for sure what was considered to be "his" thorn in the flesh. Whatever it was produced discomfort or feelings of infirmity within Paul's person. His reference to the "messenger of Satan" is certainly an indication that pain, frustration, or discomfort was a product of his thorn. The resounding message of Paul's story, "…..My grace is sufficient for you, for my strength is made perfect in weakness. …....." 2 Corinthians 12:9 NKJV. God's sufficient grace is a message I have come to appreciate in a brand new way. I have never experienced the depth of weakness that I experienced during my recovery from the "code blue." Weakness is a bitter pill for the fleshly man but it is sweet as honey for the purposes of God.

In Job and Paul's experiences, the general lesson one can take away is that at any given time we may become subject to satanic infirmities. Satan is more than willing to come into our lives as an uninvited guest. Satan desires to create as much havoc and discomfort as possible. However, God is never far away and He is always in control for His glory! The truths that are revealed through the examples of these two men inspires me to try and reconcile exactly what happened to me on the first leg of this journey. They inspire all us as we have witnessed these fascinating revelations from God.

As Bev and I began our round of golf, on the small executive (9 hole) golf course that day, I never dreamed I was about to come face to face with my first divine appointment of this entire ordeal. On the third hole, God's messenger showed up. He did not appear in visual form or in an audible voice. He was not in the wind as it blew or any aspect of the weather that day. Instead, He showed up as a pain in my side.

I stepped up on the tee box with my trusty Taylor-Made five wood. I teed the ball, got aligned addressing the ball, and made my swing. Shortly afterward, I started feeling an unusual stinging in my right side but did not think too much of it. At my age, you become accustomed to this sort of thing and go on about your business…..and so I did. I went on to play my usual lackluster round of golf, hitting enough good shots to keep me wanting to play. Those of you who attempt to play this impossible game are familiar with what I mean. The burning sensation I was feeling in my side did not go away. The pain continued and became more prominent as time passed.

Five weeks have now passed since our golf round and I am back at work. I am out at one of our rework lines and I am checking for defects. As I push the tote onto the conveyors, I still feel this nagging pain in my side. This pain has not left since the first day on the golf course, in fact, it seemed to be worsening. I made the decision that most men have a really hard time making. I decided I needed to go to the doctor and have this thing checked out. There had been plenty of time for it to subside. I was concerned that it was possibly a stress fracture to a rib. My wife thought it could be my gall bladder. I scheduled an appointment with Dr. Swan, my family physician.

It just "so happened" Dr. Swan had recently acquired an ultrasound machine for his office and was waiting for technical support on its operation. After an examination, he determined a further look with the ultrasound would be the appropriate course of action. A few days later the ultrasound was performed. I then waited patiently in the waiting room to be called back to get the results. Almost immediately, after I arrived in the treatment room, Dr. Swan showed up. I knew as soon as I saw him something was not right. His typical smile and the usual gleam in his eyes were overcast by a very serious look…..a look of dread. I knew immediately that whatever he was about to say would not be good news. I was correct!

As the doctor began to describe what the ultrasound had revealed, I felt a flood of fear as my body was overwhelmed with shock. This news was the last thing I expected to hear! After all, I felt fine other than the nuisance pain I had been feeling which by now had almost completely disappeared. I tried my best to focus and not allow my mind to run wild as the doctor explained what he had seen. It was a mass at the head of my pancreas. It was large enough for concern and further testing was required to determine the exact nature and make-up of the mass. He understood that regardless of the eventual diagnosis, to determine whether malignancy was present, the mass would need to be surgically removed. If not, it would impede the ability of the pancreas to perform its normal function of producing insulin to control blood sugar levels as well as other functions. It is amazing how such a small organ can be so vital to life. I am sure he was aware that pancreatic cancer is very seldom discovered early enough to be effectively treated. Pancreatic cancer is a very silent and very deadly cancer.

I thank God that this is a fact unknown to me at the time. In his wisdom Dr. Swan allowed me the time to let the news soak in and hope for the best. Instead, he defined for me the course of action we were going to take including an immediate trip to Memorial Hospital for an endoscopic ultrasound analysis to determine the nature of the mass. Dr. Swan recommended Dr. Charles Portera, Jr. (Dr. Portera) to me as a potential candidate to perform the surgery. Dr. Swan also scheduled a CT scan and an MRI at our local hospital. At the time, our local hospital was named Skyridge Medical Center. It has now changed to Tennova. Before the end of the day, the diagnostic planning process was in full swing. To say the least, I left the office stunned that evening. I sat in the truck awhile before heading back to work.

After work, I sat in the truck to think for a while before I turned it toward home. My worry now was how I was going to tell Bev, my wonderful wife! I knew she would not be satisfied with any answer I could give her until all was fully disclosed. Being a nurse for almost twenty-eight years, Bev would not be fooled. I decided to give her the facts as I knew them. She was aware that I had the results of the scan and I knew it would be the first thing she would want to talk about. I was correct.

Bev was in the kitchen making dinner when I got home that evening and of course the first question out of her mouth was, "What did the doctor say?" I answered by telling her it was not my gallbladder as she had first thought. I followed by telling her the doctor had found a mass on my pancreas. I added, "We may be in for a bit of a fight!" In hindsight, I had no idea how prophetic the statement was. As the following three months unfolded, I found myself in the fight of my life…..for my life. I could tell from the look on her face she knew immediately it was very serious. I suppose she read me, as I had read Dr. Swan a few hours earlier. I was totally unprepared for her response as I shared with her the initial diagnosis. This lady, who was typically a tower of strength, "lost it" for a few minutes. She was as unprepared for this news as I had been when I first received it. I must admit, based on her response, for a few minutes I thought I was as good as dead. With her medical background, she knew the normal outcome for pancreatic cancer and at that moment she could not contain her fear. For now, the issue at hand was out on the table and all we could do was stand there in the kitchen holding each other and cry. In a typical manly show of strength I interrupted the somber scene by grabbing a plate and announcing, "Time To Eat!" I ate a little…..she did not. She could only cry for the rest of the evening.

Later that night, as we prepared for bed, we had the time to allow it all to soak in and was doing a pretty good job of preparing ourselves for whatever lay ahead. I was much more comforted now that she had overcome the initial shock. She had assumed the posture of strength and support I had expected. As we lay there that evening holding each other, we had no way of knowing that we had experienced the first of many miracles we were to receive over the next few weeks.

Social Media-Legacy of Prayer and Faith:

Posted by: Tara Karis Oakes – Sept. 6th, 2013 Chattanooga Tn.

Update on Daddy.....Words cannot express our gratitude for the outpouring of love, encouragement, & prayers received today. PLEASE KEEP THEM COMING!

I'm at a loss for words so I will start by sharing what the medical staff has confirmed today. Daddy is a miracle!!! Long story short: as a result of massive blood clots blocking both lungs, Daddy's heart went into overdrive, ultimately giving out. The code team performed chest compressions for more than thirty minutes and were preparing to call time of death when the great physician interceded and restarted his heart!!! HALLELUJAH!!! PRAISE HIS HOLY NAME!!!

He is still on a ventilator in critical condition, but his vitals have steadily improved throughout the day. He is obviously aware of our presence during visiting hours and has been responsive with various movements of his face, arms, legs, and head nodding.

The primary concerns (i.e. prayer request) now are that he will not develop any bleeds due to the high levels of blood thinners, rest/comfort/peace, and that his vitals will continue to stabilize. Also, please lift up Beverly and the rest of our amazing family, especially for rest and renewal.

Thank you just doesn't seem adequate right now, but please know that every prayer has been felt. We love you all!

- With Beverly Rollins Dunn and Justin Dunn at Memorial Hospital

The events of that day marked a paradigm shift in my thinking about life and death. I did not know it at the time but I would never think about death the same again. For now, things were dark, scary, and very uncertain but we had our hope and trust in the Lord. He was truly able to bring calm to our storm.

As I look back on this episode, I find myself trying to imagine the divine activity taking place on our behalf to bring about the diagnosis of our issue. I can imagine God on His throne on a day when His sons (angels) have come before Him. I can imagine Him calling one of them before Him to give him a special assignment. I wish I could see the look on his face or hear his messengers response when the Father says, "I want you to go down and meet my servant Tony, at hole number three on a little golf course in Destin, Florida. After he hits his drive, I want you to put your finger right here.....pointing to his right side. I want you to keep it there and be a nuisance pain to him for as long as it takes him to eventually go to the doctor. My servant Dr. Swan will know what to do from there." I can only imagine what may be running through the divine messenger's mind as he leaves the presence of God. Maybe he knows what God is about to do or maybe he is simply being obedient. He could be totally unaware of the bigger plan altogether but is willing to complete his unusual mission. Either way, he was incredibly effective. More than two months would pass before I would see Dr. Swan again. This would be after my surgery for the removal of the pancreatic mass and after the ensuing "code blue."

On my first visit after being discharged from the hospital, Dr. Swan looked at me with a smile and with great emphasis states, "You know the pain you felt in your side which first brought you in for evaluation had nothing to do with the mass on your pancreas?" It was something totally separate! You would have never felt the mass growing on your pancreas!" The pain I was feeling was the first divine intervention and we both knew it. We were thanking God for it. The divine messenger had faithfully completed his task. The first of many miracles to come had been accomplished flawlessly on our behalf.

"As surely as this beauty becomes clear, it is not long
until the shadows begin to creep over the horizon
and the sun sinks in the west, leaving nothing but
darkness. The shadows, at least for a time, prevail! We
are powerless to prevent it. This is the way of death."

Chapter Two

Miracle Two, a Visit from the Dark Angel

A Season of Darkness

Yea though I walk through the valley of the shadow of Death...............

My heart is heavy today, November 18, 2014, for the loss of a dear pastor friend and the grieving family he left behind. This morning, he succumbed to the terrible disease of cancer and passed on to eternity. Although I only really knew him for a brief vapor of time, he touched my heart with the wisdom, wit, and deep unfeigned love he had for people and for Christ. He was fifty years old and a pastor of a thriving church in Middle Tennessee. He was a husband, a father of three children, and was loved by many.

My mind has been drawn to another friend whose young daughter recently departed this world by the hand of this disease. I am deeply moved by the struggles of yet another friend who was recently diagnosed with stage four in-operable cancer. He has begun chemo treatments in hopes the huge tumor can be shrunk enough to give him a chance at other corrective treatments. I find myself opening my heart and bearing it once again to the Creator, to petition Him on behalf of them and their remaining family. God is once again repeating the truths He has proclaimed so clearly over the past year and a half to me.

Life, as good as it can be, in totality is a mere valley experience. It allows us the opportunity to look upon the sunshine soaked hillsides and see the beauty of all that God has made and all that He has provided us for miles and miles. As we sit beside the ocean, we are allowed to feel the warmth of the sun's rays. We listen to the waves as they crash on to the shoreline. He helps us to feel secure and at peace with all He has created for us but eventually, the cool of the evening and then the coldness of the night grip our world.

As surely as this beauty becomes clear, it is not long until the shadows begin to creep over the horizon and the sun sinks in the west, leaving nothing but darkness. The shadows prevail, at least for a time! We are powerless to prevent it. This is the way of death. As good as life can be, these things are a reminder that death is never too far away. We can choose to live and ignore this truth as many have or we can choose to live and embrace it! To embrace it means we have to overcome a very prevalent emotion residing in us all. Too many times this emotion dominates our thoughts and actions. We must defeat FEAR!

(Ps 23:4 NKJV).....I will fear no evil......

Fear is one of the most prominent emotions preventing us from realizing the fullness of the blessings of God and His salvation. The natural enemy of life is death and our natural response to death is fear. As the scripture states, we do indeed live most of our lifetime in bondage to the fear of death. We naturally relate death to evil since death came upon humanity as a result of evil. Because of our unwillingness to obey God, we have made the choice to yield to satanic influences. This is the ultimate formula for death and destruction!

As human beings, we attempt to receive the truth of God in its fullness and then live in such a way that we are no longer subject to this fear. This is exactly how God wants us to live. The life He has given to us extends far beyond the day we lay this fleshly body in the grave. The life force of the body, which is the soul, is eternal and in God it is secure. Natural death cannot touch it. If the soul is secured in the Masters hand, there is no reason for fear.

It is this truth which adds emphasis to the importance of being born again. Being born again is the very act of submitting our soul back to God and then trusting it to His care. It is an exceedingly wicked thing we do if we take this life God has provided us and choose to live in such a way that we never honor the life giver. We take this precious gift and squander it on our petty and immoral desires without thought of the consequences. To disregard the rightful ownership of God and attempt to be the master of our own fate is the ultimate rebellion and evil. This condition will lead our soul directly to its demise which is an eternity separated from the God who made it. The only right course is one that is moving us heavenward. Through a soul that is yielded and then empowered to accomplish amazing things in Christ. Fear cannot take place. There is no capacity for it in a life such as this.

> (Ps.23:4 NKJV).....Your rod and Your
> staff, they comfort me. ...

How is it we find it so easy to live life as though we are living it alone? Why do we retreat into the shadows as though no one sees or cares? Is it not when we become so self-engulfed that we begin to make choices which sometimes gradually, and sometimes radically, lead us off course and into places of trouble? In truth, a child of God never retreats alone. If we choose to retreat, we take God with us. This is not a place God wants to be nor is it a place He wants any of us to be. To force God into retreat is like trying to mix scalding hot oil with ice cold water.....it is not going to happen. We should be prepared for divine reaction. With or without our approval, and to our shame, God will respond to bring about His plan.

We cannot deny that life is difficult and sometimes scary. Doing the right thing is never the easy thing. There is always a cost to taking a stand against the evils that are pervading into our lives and into the lives of those we love. It is a cost God expects us to be willing to pay. It is not that we yield up our own treasures for we do not own treasure. Treasure has simply been loaned to us to use for His purposes. Everything we have was loaned to us from the treasure house of heaven. In other words, God has given us treasure and He expects us to give it away. Like the manna in the wilderness, it is not made to store up for hard times.

As we walk this road, there are two things of particular significance....His Rod and His Staff. His rod can be an offensive or defensive weapon but the most prominent purpose is to help guide the sheep to their chosen destination. It is an aid to guide the sheep in the direction they should go in order to prevent them from falling into dangerous places. It enables us to deter the wild beasts when they come to pounce and do us harm. The staff on the other hand is a defensive weapon. It provides us stability and enables us to accomplish our task. It assists us when scaling through the rocky places in life and helps us to maintain a steady foothold. It is a source of comfort when the pathway gets rocky and slippery and we need stability to stand. When these two provisions are well used, they are a source of security and safety in the lives of those who learn to wield them.....those who are well trained by the Master.

> (Ps 23:6 NKJV)....Surely goodness and mercy
> shall follow me all the days of my life, and I
> will dwell in the house of the Lord forever!

In God's house there is much treasure to be found! Not the treasure we value from our worldly perspective but rather the things we know deep down in our hearts are really precious. Unfortunately for us, it can take many years and a multitude of heartbreaks and failures before we can finally grasp hold of these treasures. We are left looking back in regret, wondering why it took us so long to see. Why did I allow my desires and actions to hurt so many? Why was I so selfish that I could not sacrifice more of myself so that someone else would have an easier road to walk? Why did I give up on the ones I loved when they needed me so badly?

Things like love, compassion, and selflessness are only the beginning of the treasures found in the Lord's house. The natural effect of obtaining these gifts is a life characterized by "goodness and mercy." It is no wonder the psalmist would conclude, "I will dwell in the house of the Lord forever." Inside God's house is the stuff that makes life beautiful and fulfilling. Without first knowing Christ, it is something so radically different that human beings do not have the capacity to imagine it. Unfortunately, those who do not know this truth will never know it unless they decide to come inside the house of the Lord.

Few of us are ever prepared to come face to face with the dark and scary side of life. This is the place where we first come to realize and accept the truth concerning the brevity of our life and the fact life can end at any time. It seems we always expect bad things will happen to everyone else, while always finding a way to skip over us. I am not sure why this is. I suppose it is a built-in self-defense mechanism helping us to keep our focus on living. It prevents us from developing a morbid outlook and obsession over the truth of deaths reality.

It is much healthier from a psychological perspective and it is far better to focus on living than to focus on dying. Who wants to hang out with the person who is always talking about or focused on their fear of death? As a result of this slanted approach to living, we are usually unprepared for a visit from the reality of death…..the death angel!

As we faced the diagnostic process for this thing growing inside of me, fear became the first life reality. Suddenly, fear arrested me and entered the picture in a way like I had never known, experienced, or expected. I was forced to decide how I must deal with it. I came to develop a whole new understanding and appreciation for those who had walked this road before me. I thought I understood what they were dealing with…..I thought I could empathize with their fears…..I thought I understood the doubts running rampant through their mind.....I was wrong. This chapter is dedicated to those who have had to set and wait and helplessly wonder what the final prognosis would be.

I can assure you, you will never know a fear such as this. You will never feel more vulnerable or more unbearably anxious! As we reflect on this stage of my journey, I have chosen the following scriptures to help you realize that first moment of fear. I hope it serves to help you understand the inner turmoil going through a person's mind when he or she comes face to face with the death angel. I hope it helps you to be prepared when this unwelcomed visitor shows up on your doorstep.....as he most certainly will one day. It may come with some measure of fore-warning or it may come suddenly with no warning at all. It will most certainly come.

Social Media-Legacy of Prayer and Faith:

Posted by: Brooke Studdard Epperson – Sept 7th, 2013

Father I come to you right now at 4:53 in the morning burdened. I pray for your healing hand to be placed on Tony and for your hand of peace to be placed on Beverly and their family. We know that when we come to the throne and ask, you hear our prayer! The things that we cannot understand you not only know but you have walked before us and your faithfulness to us never fails. Lord I love you and am thankful for the blessings this far. Amen Hebrews 13:8

Beverly Rollins Dunn, Tara Karis Oakes, Carrie McAmis, and 7 others like this.

When Death Reveals Itself!

Ps 55:4-6 (NKJV) 4 My heart is severely pained within me, and the terrors of death have fallen upon me.5

> Fearfulness and trembling have come upon me, And horror has overwhelmed me. 6 So I said, "Oh, that I had wings like a dove! I would fly away and be at rest.

I had now been given a new knowledge. I had something growing inside me that could potentially end my life. I found myself confused, afraid, doubtful, and depressed. I wondered what the final outcome would be. Would I soon be saying farewell to my beautiful wife and children? Would I say farewell to others that I had come to love as I made this journey along life's pathway? Would my remaining days be filled with pain, weakness, hospital visits, and deterioration until there was nothing left of me? Would I be able to maintain my faith and strength of character in a way that leaves my family and friends feeling blessed and happy to be a child of God?

These and many other questions find their way into the mind of a person who has had an intimate introduction to the death angel. We have spent our whole lifetime trying to avoid this encounter, but it is now a reality. Like the psalmist, I found myself wishing I could deny the facts and fly away to somewhere more pleasant. Oh how I wished there was somewhere else I could go to escape the unknown. The fear gripping my life made me ashamed. I was ashamed because I had thought when this day came I would be prepared…..I was not. At least for now, I thought faith in God would win the day. It did not. This horrible fear was choking me. I tried with all my might to cover it up and be strong. I did not want others to know my fear. I think it may be a "man thing" to cover up the true content of the heart. At the time, it seemed the right thing to do. I felt if I acknowledged the possible negative outcomes they would become a self-fulfilling prophecy. So…..I ignored them.

I realize now, in this moment in time, God gave me a gift of calmness as the storm began to rage on every front. God helped me to see the fears and doubts on the faces of those I love. I was overcome with desire to be strong and to help them be strong. It is a supernatural thing when we are given the strength to look beyond ourselves. It is one of the most basic gifts of Christ and especially in the example He personally provided. It is only when we can see beyond ourselves that we can find true peace, power, passion, and comfort from our divine master. He has such a hard time blessing us when we spend our time in worry, self-pity, and fearfulness.

Although I was overwhelmed in every sense of the word, I became confident that somehow it would work out for the best. I had no idea exactly how this would end—somehow I knew it would be alright. I think this feeling of certainty may be the greatest blessing that faith provides. After all, of life's many uncertainties, death is not one of them. We all have an appointed time when we will take our very last breath. What really matters is that we know who controls our eternity and holds our next breath in His hands. This is one thing I never doubted.

Overcoming the Overwhelming

> Heb 2:14-15 NKJV "14 Inasmuch then as the children have partaken of flesh and blood, He Himself likewise shared in the same, that through death He might destroy him who had the power of death, that is, the devil, 15 and release those who through fear of death were all their lifetime subject to bondage."

It is a difficult lesson to accept! This physical body of ours is flawed and will one day cease to provide the fleshly home for our spirit to inhabit. Our physical life does not come with a guarantee to last sixty, seventy, or eighty years. However, we assume it will. We are so naïve! Medicine is a wonderful thing. This is a truth I had come to appreciate through its application in those days of distress. Medicine can only go so far.

Social Media-Legacy of Prayer and Faith:

Posted by: Tara Karis Oakes – Sept 7th, 2013 Chattanooga Tn.

Specific prayers needed for Daddy today:

1. No Brain or surgical bleeds
2. Continued breaking up of blood clots (including new one in leg)
3. Blood pressure stabilization

4. Kidney Function
5. Pain management/comfort/rest

Please see my previous post for more details on his condition and feel free to share any and all updates. We need all the prayers we can get. Sincerest thanks again for all the support.

■ With Clyde Dunn, and 2 others at Memorial Hospital

There are things that will arise unexpectedly in our lives. We may then discover that medicine has no power over them. At that point, we will be left to fully focus on faith and divine will. Our lives are in God's hand and He alone decides the outcome. This truth, when accepted and allowed to pass from the mind to the heart, becomes the most liberating truth in the life of the believer. Our lives have always been kept in the hands of the Creator. We have a tendency to forget this.

I am thankful for the example God has provided for us all through His son, Jesus Christ. His example should encourage us when we find ourselves walking through the valley of the shadow of death. Truly one of the greatest mysteries and special blessings is how God became flesh and endured the same afflictions that common men endure. The greatest example was when Christ faced the shame of the crucifixion. Because of His Son, God has a personal understanding of our fear and terror of death. I assure you, God heard as Jesus prayed in the garden of Gethsemane as He ask God to let the cup pass from Him if possible.

For the completion of salvation's plan, unfortunately for Jesus this was not possible. The Father is constantly reminded when He views the scars on His Son who is seated at His right hand. He understands the grief we bear when those we love slip away in the night and we find their lifeless corpse in the morning. He understands the grief we feel as we hold the hand of a dying mother and we hear the last breath and see the last tear drop come from her eyes. He knows the anguish we feel when we pick up the phone to learn a special someone we love so dearly has perished as the result a terrible accident. God knows the anguish we feel as we watch someone slowly leave us because of the terrible disease that is overwhelming their body. God the Father knows this because His Son experienced death firsthand. Therefore, God has experienced death firsthand.

We should never forget what God has done for us. God allowed His Son to become an object of shame on Golgotha's hill. He allowed Jesus, to be ridiculed and beaten, to be mocked by wicked men, and then to die. Yes, He had the power to raise Jesus up anew. The Father had to turn His face away from His precious Son while wicked, demon filled men, released the fury of hell upon Him. I cannot imagine the pain the Father endured as the Son felt the lashes tearing the flesh from His bones. I cannot begin to understand the grace that kept God from demanding immediate retribution from those who murdered Jesus. Instead of wrath, God heard His perfect Lamb petitioning Him to "forgive them"! With His last breath, this was Jesus last request….. And then He tasted death for us all.

I cannot help but think about the scene in the garden of Gethsemane. Jesus went a little farther and fell on His face and prayed, "O My Father, if it is possible, let this cup pass from Me; nevertheless, not as I will, but as You will." (Matt 26:39 NKJV) It was at this point He faced the fear that we will all eventually face! It was here He looked the death angel in the eye, giving him permission to take Him. The death angel would never have power over our Lord if it had not been given to him. It is here our hope springs its highest. It is here we, as believers, can let go of the fear of death and the grip it holds over us in this life.

Because our Lord lives and broke the curse of death, we can all live. For the child of God, the grave holds no victory and death holds no sting. It is a certainty of faith. I have encountered a small taste of the "peace" that passes all understanding. I know there is something beautiful awaiting those who simply believe, in faith, and have placed their trust in Christ alone.

When we begin to apply these amazing facts of God's love for us we can begin to put our personal lives into perspective. As though it were the first time I began to understand how amazing it is to be a child of God. We cannot possibly understand the victory over the grave until we know the transforming power in the salvation of our souls.

Our soul can never be safe until we willingly return it to the Father who created it. It is God and God alone who can preserve it, sustain it, and bring glory from it. I have absolutely no doubt that our Heavenly Father, through Jesus, has defeated death once and for all…..for us all! In His hand He holds both the blackness of death and the marvelous light of truth and power. He exercises full control over them both for our benefit.

Social Media-Legacy of Prayer and Faith:

Posted by: Carrie McAmis – Sept.7th, 2013

Beverly, I am praying for you and the whole family, for complete healing and no further complications and for strength for you all. We serve a MIGHTY GOD!!! We have already seen so many miracles.

I knew these things in my mind before I met this unwelcomed visitor. I experienced them anew in my heart when I was allowed to see the Lord exercise His domination in them. For fifty-five minutes, when there was no breath in my body, God was there! For fifty-five minutes, I felt a peace that cannot be understood or properly explained. He held my soul in His hands. He left me no room for doubt or for fear.

Many have asked me what I saw during the fifty-five minutes when there was no heart- beat. They seem a little disappointed when I tell them I did not see anything. Many people seem to have a curiosity about the infamous "divine light". It was not what I saw but it was what I heard and felt that left its mark on my being. I felt an indescribable peace! I heard calm and soothing voices. I have felt a powerful presence and fearlessness ever since…..it was not there before. It is clear to me now that this thing did not happen to give me something sensational to talk about. However, it is absolutely sensational. As my surgeon, Dr. Portera said during a follow-up visit recently, "How can you embellish on an event such as this? The facts are sensational enough!"

God has come near and He has changed my life as well as the lives of others. Many of our perspectives are forever changed. He has given me courage, a confidence, and a faith that I could never have gotten any other way. This is the true miracle of it all. Maybe now, God can use me as He has planned all along.

God Comes Calling

Isa 38:1-2 (NKJV)

1 In those days Hezekiah was sick and near death. And
Isaiah the prophet, the son of Amoz, went to him and said
to him, "Thus says the LORD: 'Set your house in order,
for you shall die and not live.'"2 Then Hezekiah turned
his face toward the wall, and prayed to the LORD,

The story of King Hezekiah has always fascinated me. King H was a good
king, one who feared the Lord and did what was right. He was an example
of faith and he refused to abandon the Lord when the odds seemed to be
stacked against him. He was truly a man God loved. Hezekiah was blessed,
and as a result, he was allowed to experience the healing hand of God in
a very special way.

It was in his response to the message of the angel of death, delivered by
the prophet Isaiah, that we can learn the most about Hezekiah's character
but most importantly the character and purpose of God. For most people,
the visit of the death angel catches them totally unaware. The message of
the death angel is irrevocable. This was not the case for Hezekiah. In his
story, there are many lessons all believers would do well to learn.

We should consider the visit and the message from Isaiah. This message
was made up of three major components. First of all, Isaiah's message was
one that was uttered by the mouth of the Lord. Isaiah was merely repeating
it in Hezekiah's presence. Secondly, it was a call for Hezekiah to set his
house in order. This was a warning very few people ever receive. There
are many who go into eternity leaving a lifetime of unfinished business,
broken hearts, words unsaid, and lives untouched. Finally, it was a message
of authority and finality.

Hezekiah's life had been threatened by his enemies many times, but
none of those threats could compare to this. God declared Hezekiah's
death sentence. Hezekiah knew God held both life and death in His
hands, and God was fully able to perform His will. Hezekiah's response
was prayer, a petition for God to wait. He responded with tears. Hezekiah
loved the life that God had blessed him with, and he wanted to continue

for God's glory. The impact of his faith was instantaneous, for Isaiah soon returned with the answer Hezekiah was seeking.

Hezekiah's Responds by Writing

Isaiah 38:9—20 (NKJV) This is the writing of Hezekiah king of Judah, when he had been sick and had recovered from his sickness: 10 I said, "In the prime of my life I shall go to the gates of Sheol; I am deprived of the remainder of my years."11 I said, "I shall not see YAH, The LORD in the land of the living; I shall observe man no more among the inhabitants of the world.12 My life span is gone, Taken from me like a shepherd's tent; I have cut off my life like a weaver. He cuts me off from the loom; from day until night You make an end of me. 13 I have considered until morning — like a lion, So He breaks all my bones; from day until night You make an end of me. 14 Like a crane or a swallow, so I chattered; I mourned like a dove; my eyes fail from looking upward. O LORD, I am oppressed; Undertake for me! 15 "What shall I say? He has both spoken to me, and He Himself has done it. I shall walk carefully all my years in the bitterness of my soul. 16 O Lord, by these things men live; And in all these things is the life of my spirit; so, You will restore me and make me live. 17 Indeed it was for my own peace that I had great bitterness; but You have lovingly delivered my soul from the pit of corruption, For You have cast all my sins behind Your back. 18 For Sheol cannot thank You, Death cannot praise You; Those who go down to the pit cannot hope for Your truth.19 The living, the living man, he shall praise You, As I do this day; The father shall make known Your truth to the children.20 "The LORD was ready to save me; Therefore we will sing my songs with stringed instruments All the days of our life, in the house of the LORD."

As I re-read this passage after I was released from the hospital. I was arrested by the fact that Hezekiah had described feeling the same emotions I had experienced after first learning of my diagnosis. I could relate to Hezekiah in a way I never could have before. As he described his feelings, (verse 10-15), it was amazing to me the similarities in his reaction to my own. He worried he had been cut down before living the fullness of his days. He thought about all those he knew and loved and fretted about being separated from them. He wondered at how he would deteriorate and suffer before finally succumbing to the death angel.

It is important for us to remember these things were written after he had received his healing. I think it is very important for us to stop and consider his message. I think one of his motives for writing was simply to describe for us the thought process, reactions to the fears occurring at the moment a person realizes their death could be imminent. This message contains three truths about Hezekiah's mindset. The first message, he had a desire to write and share his experience. His second message, he was willing to honestly expose the fears and doubts he faced as a result of receiving a death sentence. And the third message, he wanted people to know his confidence in God and his thankfulness for the healing and restorative power he had experienced.

First of all, Hezekiah desired to write and share his experience. After receiving his healing from the Lord, he could not contain his joy and thankfulness that God had heard and responded to his prayers. He was compelled to share the entirety of his experience. He shared every part of his experience including the parts that would cause shame for most of us, as I am sure it did for him as well. I believe he had pure motives for writing. Hezekiah wanted to glorify his God. He wanted to share his feelings of desperation and to proclaim his thankfulness for the healing power of God. I believe he understood many would read his words afterward and find great comfort in them as I did. This is one of the amazing things about God's Word. The truths it introduces to us are timeless and never lose their power.

The second truth of his reaction is his willingness to share honestly his feelings and emotions upon learning of his soon demise. We should remember this is a king. Many men, in like positions of power, would have found it very difficult to describe and share their feelings of weakness and

despair. Hezekiah not only shared them, he shared them in detail. I believe
he understood these are the fears every person must come to deal with at
some point in their life. I think he wanted us to understand that position
and station in life is insignificant when it comes to the end of our days.
Death will visit us all. I can certainly relate to the despair he shared with
us, and I am sure there are many others who can relate as well.

The third component of his writing comes in the form of praises to his
God. He understood his life was in the hands of a far greater, far mightier
king than himself. It was his proclamation of faith that has brought
peace and consolation to so many who have faced the prospect of death
in a very real and powerful way. Hezekiah had a heart full of praise and
thanksgiving to a God who was able to arrest the death angel and stay his
hand. Not many of us get to see this deliverance in a real, life altering way.
This passage was one I could not omit. In my own simple way, I would
like to share with you the feelings of joy and thankfulness that fill my
heart and life today.

The first motive I have for writing today is praise. I have seen God in
a way I had never dreamed possible, and I must share it. My secondary
motive is to warn those who may read this message. In the section below,
Jeremiah makes an appeal to every believer to make the most of the time
God has allotted you. This warning is not for believers only, it is a call to
unbelievers as well. There may come a time when the truths I share come
to resonate in your life. The Lord is Lord of all.....even of unbelievers.
Every life has been uniquely ordered by the Lord. There is no other person
qualified to accomplish what God has chosen for you. Be obedient to His
purpose for your life!

Redeeming Your Time

Jer.13:15-16 (NKJV)

15 Hear and give ear: Do not be proud, For the LORD
has spoken. 16 Give glory to the LORD your God before
He causes darkness, and before your feet stumble on the
dark mountains, And while you are looking for light,

He turns it into the shadow of death And makes it dense darkness.

I have never considered myself an overly proud or arrogant person. I had many things to learn as God began to reveal these things that were so far beyond my control. I have realized that average people live with a certain amount of unbridled pride, and it serves as a barrier to their relationship with God and others. We all make assumptions we are "in control".....we are not and never have been. This is especially true if we are attempting to live a life of faith and dependence upon the Lord.

If we are not watchful, pride can become a barrier preventing us from hearing the voice of God and will eventually put us on a collision course with His divine will. Jeremiah understood this. This is why he exhorted those reading his words to put away their pride and to enable them to hear the Word of the Lord. The person who successfully keeps pride at bay in their life will find an open door for bringing glory to God. This was Jeremiah's second point.

What is our Christian experience really all about? Is it not to bring glory to an amazing God? Should we not live a life that reveals and exemplifies His power to the world? As Christians, too many times we allow the difficulties and trials of life to overwhelm us, making it extremely difficult to bring glory to an all-powerful God. God is truly worthy of honor!

When I read the passage above, it reminds me to do a check-up. Has my life and does my life bring glory to God? What have I spent my time doing? Have I been more interested in bringing glory to myself? Have I focused too much on accomplishing the things I feel are most important to me without giving due consideration to His divine purposes for my life? Have I overcome the fears and doubts that often come to the surface, causing me to drift from the divine course? These are all questions I find myself asking today. I can look back and see how great and awesome God has shown himself on my behalf. I am afraid I have failed miserably at giving Him His due praises and at living the kind of life that shows His power. This is a mistake that I have no intention of continuing to make. According to Jeremiah, I am not guaranteed an infinite amount of time to accomplish God's will in my life. I should stop living as though I do! We should all take heed!

Jeremiah spoke about a day of darkness in his writing. It is not a darkness encroaching upon us by pure coincidence. Instead, it is a darkness deliberately brought on by the Lord. We should not assume this is a punishment for disobedience, although it certainly can be. We should receive it for what it is. In the spirit of this entire chapter, we should hear clearly. The Lord has a day of darkness set aside for us all.

This is the day when life can no longer find a way. It is a day when the thing most of us have spent our entire lifetime dreading becomes a reality. It is a day when all of our actions, good or evil, will be brought before our eyes. Our strength will become weakness when we stand before the Mighty One as He judges the entirety of our life. Although justice seems a foreign concept in the modern age in which we live, it will not be foreign on this day. God's justice will reign supreme.

In conclusion, some may wonder how it is I can consider this initial revelation a miracle. After all, we all know deep down we are going to die one day. We are all going to meet the death angel. But for me, I must consider this revelation a miracle. God took what had previously been only knowledge in my mind to the place where it became a reality in my life and in my heart. He made death personal and real for me! Through His demonstration of the power to deliver me from death, He humbled me. He crushed my spirit of self-sufficiency. I know, literally, He holds my very next breath in His mighty hands. There will come another day when I feel the last breath leave my body to never return. He expanded my capacity for compassion by allowing me to experience a horrible fear and doubt such as I had never known.

Therefore, I now have a much greater understanding of what others feel when facing similar circumstances. God painted a tapestry of love in the lives of my family and friends. Somehow, I knew it was there all along, but it had not been realized or appreciated. Now, I can see it much more clearly. I could probably go on forever realizing and recounting the many gifts God gave me through this first encounter. It is hard to imagine there would be more encounters to come…..but there were! Hold on!

Chapter Three

Miracle Three, My Angels and My Friends

From left to right Dr. Charles Portera Jr., Michael
Sullivan, Bill Bolton, Tony (Lydell) Dunn, Brian Sax,
Brooke Kelly, Deanna Hopkins, and Mariamma Varghese.
Front, Ruth Lightsey and Amber Forster Simpson.

Puppets, People, and Living Souls

Puppetry holds a great mystery concerning the nature of people! Although I have never held all that much interest in puppetry, as a child or a man, I am finding it more intriguing all the time. Think about it, a puppet is a character that can be seen by the natural eye but whose life force comes from an unseen hand. We see it move and we hear it speak. It is not the puppet moving and speaking, but rather the voice and hand of the person holding it. When I see the puppet in this light, it opens up a mystery within man and puts the human experience in a whole new perspective. The biblical creation account of humanity has a very special message in light of the puppetry revelation.

In the beginning, God created us! Man did not become a living body, but he became a living soul as stated in the Genesis description! Why was this? I believe God never intended to put first preference on the body. It is merely the part of our existence that can be seen with the natural eye. It is no more alive than the puppet without the hand of the puppeteer. Instead, He referred to us as "living souls" because the soul is the hand of the puppeteer. It is God who fills our body. I realize this concept flies in the face of those who have invested their resources to achieve personal beauty! Maintaining the youthful beauty of this body is impossible. Like a garment, it will wear out and grow old.

When we consider the soul, the life force, we see the divine that has been placed inside this earthen vessel. It never loses its beauty or its power. In fact, the spiritual man grows and becomes more prevalent. It controls our words and then our actions. If we have acknowledged the Creator who gave it to us as a gift and are living in such a way as to please Him, then our soul will live in unity with His purposes. Our body will also remain under His control. The things we do and the things we say will reflect His nature and be a blessed encouragement and strength to all those we touch.

We must realize not every human being accepts the fact that this life force within them is a divine gift. In fact, they do not want to acknowledge divinity at all. To them, there is nothing divine about it. It is all a natural, randomly occurring phenomenon, and their life has no divine purpose or power at all. I find this concept extremely sad. If they can never see beyond their humanism, it will eventually result in the destruction of their soul.

The result, the Creator's hand cannot fill and guide their life. His hand is unwelcomed there and God will never force himself upon them. Instead, because they have rejected the presence of divinity, their lives soon become invaded by the spiritual destroyer, the satanic. The great imposter becomes their puppeteer and they yield to his words and actions. Satan will not wait for an invitation. He will barge in and set up his throne totally undetected, all the while allowing them to think they are in control.

Their life soon begins to reflect him in all his darkness and evil. It is this reality that has been my greatest challenge. I so often find myself wanting to lash out at those who perpetrate evil deceptions, destructive behaviors, and ungodly acts upon those innocents around them. The spirit must constantly remind me that those persons are merely reflecting the perversions of their puppet master. I too made this mistake before I made peace with and allowed the Creator full control in my life. We should always pray for God to reveal the source of their evil impulses that so often overwhelm them.....leaving them feeling powerless.

Jesus said, ".....for out of the abundance of the heart the mouth speaks"(Mat. 12:34 NKJV). The enemies of Jesus said of Jesus, ".....no man ever spoke like this Man"(John 7:46 NKJV). Jesus was full of holiness. When He spoke, He did not speak to the body with all the outward manifestations. Instead, He spoke with authority to the soul, to the puppet master, the source of their actions and words. His Words were a direct reflection of the Creator and spoken with the same force as that of His Father. Truth will always be truth and will always be representative of the divine power.

Understanding this has helped me recognize those who come alongside of me that are vessels showing me the mercies and power of God. How precious it is to be in the presence of those who have made God their Lord and Master and have lived yielded to Him. On the other hand, I am challenged to not condemn those who live under the power of the great deceiver, for I was there once myself. Instead, I should speak truth to their soul just as Jesus did, in accordance with the will of the Creator. This is the only solution for their troubled and unfulfilled life! "But the natural man does not receive the things of the spirit of God for they are foolishness to him, nor can he know them, because they are spiritually discerned." (1 Cor. 2:14 NKJV). Their only hope is to discover the true puppet master, the Creator of their soul. He will drive away all other imposters and fill their lives with power, peace, and purpose.

I suppose one needs to understand a little more about me in order to understand my reactions to the medical events I was being thrust into. I am a man, not unlike most. I live with an extremely independent and self-confident attitude. I do not go out of my way to meet and make new friends, as I have always had a more private disposition. It is not that I do not have friends, for I do, and they are true friends. I can count on them any time. I hope they think the same of me. They have proven their legitimacy to me and my family, over and over again, for the past several months. If fact, my heart is overwhelmed with thankfulness for them every time they cross my mind or I see them.

I have tried to avoid being a superficial kind of friend. I have also tried to avoid attracting superficial friends. There are many who have a warped perspective of true friendship and surround themselves with like-minded kinds of relationships. To them, friends are people you can use as a way to meet your own needs or accomplish some goal you have set for yourself. A relationship with them tends to be a one way street, lots of taking on their part but not much giving.

I suppose there is a place for those kind of relationships, but they should never be confused with true friendship. These superficial types of relationships tend to be with those who are business associates or a loose association of people with common interest. It is possible to develop true and deep friendships in such social arrangements. I have been blessed with several truly wonderful friends.

Social Media-Legacy of Prayer and Faith:

Posted by: Toni McFarland Goodwin – Sept 8th, 2013 Chattanooga Tn.

 **Praying over Beverly Rollins Dunn, Tara Karis Dunn, Justin Dunn, and Tony Dunn. Jeremiah 31:25 believing the Lord in His Word "I will refresh the weary and satisfy the faint."**

I am deeply thankful for those with whom I work on the job each day. They have become real and true friends. We must remember that real friendship runs deep. True friends are there for you even if there is nothing to gain by it. Real friends are willing to sacrifice for you with no expectation you will ever repay them, for they have a motive of love and nothing else. As I began this chapter, I did so with an overflowing gratitude for the many friends I have and the new friends with which I have been recently blessed. These new friends have come by way of intimate medical professionalism and the providence of Almighty God. They have not only touched my body, but also my heart.

This chapter is dedicated to my medical professional friends. I would like to give special recognition to Dr. Swan, our family physician, Dr. Charles Portera, Jr., my surgeon, his nurse Deanna Hopkins, Dr. Steciw who led the code blue efforts, Dr. Barrow, my special radiologist at Skyridge, and Dr. Brooke Daniel, who diagnosed our allergy to Heparin! They were our angels as all of the unforeseen events unfolded. These five, along with Dr. Pesce and Dr. Baleeiro, with their staff at Memorial Hospital, the nurses on the fifth floor who first responded to the saddle clot that had silently formed in my lungs, the MICU personnel who cared for me during and after the code blue, are people of excellence who do their jobs superbly every day. I believe the life-giving care they provide is not only for a paycheck, but rather because of genuine love and compassion.

I ask you to remember them in prayer as they carry on their work of healing. I pray for all the unmentioned, additional medical professionals, who touch lives with compassion every day…..day in and day out. These people will always be special to me and will hold a most special place in my heart. As many of them have shared their thoughts and perspectives, concerning their observations throughout this crisis, I have been amazed. Our lives have been touched and we now share a most special bond. It is really as much their story as it is mine.

Today is March 01, 2014. It has been one hundred and fifty-five days since my release from the hospital. Yesterday, my wife Bev and I returned to our surgeon's office for a check-up. A couple of weeks ago, I had my follow up CT scan and cancer marker blood-work. My wife and I were anxious and more than a little fretful to get the results. After a very short wait, in came our surgeon and oncologist, Dr. Portera. He was all smiles and complimentary on how well I was looking. He got right to the point by telling us the blood work and scans looked great. We both breathed a collective sigh of relief. I had no idea, as good as this news was for us, we were about to receive another huge blessing that came totally unexpectedly.

We started talking about what had been going on in our lives, as it had been almost two months since we last saw him. I shared with him how we had been encouraged to write our story and were in the process of doing so. I told him I'd love to arrange a lunch or dinner get together with him, his assistant, and their spouses. I continued by telling him I'd love to get their perspective and their feelings about all the events that had occurred, in order to better authenticate this writing. We were unprepared for what happened next. Dr. Portera's countenance changed, as though he was accessing a part of his brain that held a special memory. I am sure glad he did.

First of all, you must understand and visualize a few things about this man. He recently turned 50 years old. He stands about six feet and three or four inches tall. He is built like a professional linebacker having broad shoulders and a sturdy frame. His voice is steady, deep, and confident. Immediately after I was diagnosed, I was told by a friend, "He wears cowboy boots!" My response….."This is exactly the kind of man I want working on me!" Without apology, I can declare that I am a bit biased to the down home, common sense, country type. As I look back, there is no doubt he was the right man for this job. He was the man in whom God had chosen as my angel and agent of healing.

The experience he shared with us that day left me totally overwhelmed. It is not my intention to disclose every part of the conversation from the office that day, but I do want to share the impact of the conversation. I will share with you the revelations that came to me as I sat there listening to him. Dr. Portera recalled his thoughts and his reactions on the day I coded. He said, "You died!"

I was moved and blessed in a way that I am not sure can be adequately explained. Dr. Portera choked back tears as he spoke about that special day that had left him in awe. He described his feelings, his actions, his desperation, and then his amazement with each part of the event. He spoke of the long term impact it had on his relationship with his family and those he loves. From our conversation, it appeared to have changed his perspective as a physician.

> "As I stood in your room that day and observed as the team was performing the code, I concluded you were a dead man. I was going to have to go tell your family that you had died. As I approached the waiting room, where your family was gathered, I was unable to make myself walk through the door. There was so much grief in the room that I could not go in. I walked on past the door and went and stood in the stairwell. As I stood there arguing with God, (my interpretation of his words) suddenly I felt warmth from the top of my head to the bottom of my feet. I knew it was going to be OK. I turned and walked back past the waiting room and into your room. At this point, I observed the monitor to see as your heart-beat returned."

Needless to say, when he had finished speaking I was an emotional basket case. I went in and out of frequent lapses into tears, I could not contain them. I kept seeing him as he shared his heart through tears.

I thought, "wow, how great is a God who can arrange and orchestrate events in such a way as to meet the needs in the lives of so many, and simultaneously." Before today, I was seeing this event in a really selfish perspective. "What was God doing for, or telling me?" When Dr. Portera agreed to do the "Foreword" for this book, it was a huge blessing for Bev and me. When God brought us together for His display of divine power, beyond the physical healing, I feel God had a special purpose for Dr. Portera's family and for mine.

I had not stopped to think about the fact that I was not the only target of God's affection that day. His plans went far beyond me. It totally changed my thought process as I tried to recollect events and make plans to complete this work. The greatest challenge I now face is to gain a better understanding of what God did, and was doing, in the lives of those involved. More so, how did He use this event to impact my angels and my friends? This third miracle is really not about me as much as it is about them. I may never know the extent God used my situation to speak to the many hearts He touched that day, but I certainly want to try. I have visited with many of those involved in this event, and I have learned many things I never knew. In fact, it seems every time I talk to someone, I get a new perspective. It is so exciting to hear!

Social Media-Legacy of Prayer and Faith:

Posted by: Tara Karis Oakes – Sept. 8th, 2013 Chattanooga Tn.

Daddy's temperature did go down overnight – ANSWERED PRAYER!

NEW REQUESTS:

- **We need his platelets to go up now so he can continue on the Heparin to dissipate the clots.**
- **His creatinine decreased some overnight but needs to continue coming down.**

- They have also started his feedings, so please pray everything goes smoothly with that.
- And please say an extra prayer for rest, strength, & health for Beverly, Justin, and I (& the rest of the family)

Thanks again, all our love!

Bev and I try to make a point to visit with our special angels every chance we get. They continue to amaze us when they recall, even these many months past the event, the things which have continued to amaze them about what happened that day and beyond.

Bill Bolton, R.N., was one of the first responder caregivers and one of our nurses in MICU. I recently emailed him to set up an interview for him to share his perspective. While in MICU, Bill kept me up to date on what was going on in the golf world. Golf is a passion he and I both share. He took a few days off in his schedule to attend the PGA Championship in Atlanta. I was a bit jealous, but he told me all about it when he returned. His response to my request is typical of many of the comments we have received from so many of the medical staff.

> Bill said, "You have noted on multiple occasions how blessed you have been by all of us and the events that led our paths to cross. I am not sure you are aware of how much you have blessed me (us) in return. Not only did God allow the events of your medical treatment to unfold in the way they did, to show you the blessings He has given you, they also reminded me of how much He has blessed me too. I will always be thankful for that day, not because of what you and your family experienced, but for the fact that God used you and your family to remind me of His power and most of all God's love for us. Not only because you survived, but because you survived and gave Him the credit for surviving. We truly were only the tools and instruments He used that day."

Bill Bolton, MICU, a new golfing buddy.

During the first return visit we made to Memorial, after being discharged six weeks earlier, we went to the fifth floor where our emergency ordeal began. We spoke to several medical personnel that provided care for us. The nurse assigned to me the day of my event was Mariamma Varghese, R.N. The day of our visit Mariamma produced a document to show us. This document was the report of the saddle clot that had developed in my lungs the day of the crash. She informed us she keeps the report close and refers to it many times, especially on those days when things get rough. This document reminds her of just how much her effort can make a difference. It helps to encourage her to keep on keeping on. It is her way of recognizing and remembering what God can accomplish on behalf of His children.

Recently, after almost a year and a half, I visited the MICU. As I walked through, I did not see many familiar faces. Most days, the MICU staff does not have the time to stand around and fellowship. On this particular day, I noticed a lady sitting at the desk doing paperwork. As I walked by, she glanced up for a second and then went back to her task. I walked around the unit, and as I came around the other side, I was face to face with the lady I had seen at the workstation. She pointed at me as though I was a ghost. She immediately recognized me, but I did not immediately remember her. She introduced herself to me as Stacey Henry, R.N.

Stacey Henry   **Dianne Eure**

She explained that she had been one of the three nurses taking turns administering chest compressions when I coded that day. As she recalled the events of that day, I was amazed at the specific details she was able to recall, much the same way as listening to the recollection of others. Through tears of joy she embraced me. Once again, I was amazed at how God had brought so many special people into my life. I am still, after all this time, getting introduced to some of them. I had not seen her the many times I have visited, since my discharge, because she had been on maternity leave having a beautiful new baby.

Dr. Steciw and Me, After the Healing

On one visit, I was blessed to see Dr. Steciw. Dr. Steciw was the physician in charge of leading my code blue. While I was in the hospital, I did not get to spend much time getting to know her personally. Somehow, I know she is a uniquely special individual. On this particular day, she hugged me and smiled. She repeated to me that day, something I hear routinely to this day, especially from medical friends. She said, "God's not finished with you yet!" They do not realize, as I have not realized, how badly I need to hear this message. These words speak to so many of my insecurities and questions about God's purpose for me.

Social Media-Legacy of Prayer and Faith:

Posted by: Beverly Rollins Dunn – Sept 9th, 2013 Chattanooga Tn.

I have seen a lot of post that seem to minister to my heart from God. Please pray for specific needs. He needs to increase his platelets and maintain them. He needs to increase his hemoglobin and hematocrit. He needs to have another good decrease in his creatinine to have another good blood thinner option. General healing and recovery. He has communicated with paper and pencil when we could not understand the motions he was using. Thank you all so much and glory and praises, and honor to the Father!!

Aileen Shepphard, Carrie McAmis, Marilyn Hardin Gibson, and 20 others like this.

This affirmation was significant coming from a lady with so much obvious intelligence, and she was unafraid to credit God for His intervention. I know she was used in a mighty way during the code. She was unwilling to give up, even though standard protocol had far been exceeded. I think she knew something that no one else in the room knew at the time, she may not have been totally aware of it herself. That is the way God works! In my son's testimony, later in the book he shares his own observations about Dr. Steciw.

Sweet Nurse Alison and I, after the healing!

And then there's Alison Patterson, R.N., another one of my assigned MICU nurses. She was my assigned nurse when first admitted to the MICU. She is the first nurse I remember when I began to reemerge back into the land of the living. Every time I have seen her when returning to visit I feel the same sweet spirit and see the same brightness in her eyes. On one of my first visits, she asked me if I remembered any of those first moments after I regained consciousness. This was a time when everything was all so very vague. For a period of several days before and several days after the event, I was unable to remember specific details.

Soon after this visit, I started remembering at least one episode when she was in the room working at the bedside when I awoke. When I opened my eyes, and for just a moment, I thought she might be an angel. I could feel the love and the warmth and I felt safe. She embodies all the wonderful qualities a nurse should possess. I can feel the same warm spirit when I see her today. She exudes a powerful life force! When in her presence, I feel blessed and strengthened.

Without fail, as I have spoken with the many who were present and who provided care for me during those critical days, one common theme always emerges. Everyone involved ascribes the glory and praise to God for what happened. They realize they were vessels in the hands of the Master, and it is He who deserves the glory. They are shining examples of what can happen when we allow the hand of the truly divine Puppet Master to fill our lives.

Social Media-Legacy of Prayer and Faith:

Posted by: Beverly Rollins Dunn – Sept. 10th, 2013 Chattanooga Tn.

Update for Tony this morning. Platelets at 31000, still low but did not drop again, so they are starting him on the other blood thinner. Kidney function is back to normal at 1.0. Thank you all for continuing to stand in the gap for us. Praises to the Almighty God who proves to be so faithful to a child who falters in faith (me).

I do not know exactly what they needed on this special day, but I do know their needs were divinely provided. Some of these special angels have now moved on to new opportunities. The work they performed on my eventful day, and the things they experienced, will always be with them. The time I was blessed to spend with them will remain a cherished part of my memory. I hope to always remain close and stay in touch with them all. I look forward to seeing what God will do through them.

Social Media-Legacy of Prayer and Faith:

Posted by: Toni McFarland Goodwin – Sept. 10th, 2013

Beverly Rollins Dunn, Tara Karis Dunn, and Justin Dunn I see this verse being lived out in you and your unwavering faith. "Though the mountains be shaken and the hills be removed, yet my unfailing love for you will not be shaken nor my covenant of peace be removed," says the Lord, who has compassion on you. (Isaiah 54:10 NIV)

So now, as I try to reconcile this life I have been blessed with, I am challenged to look upon those with whom I may cross paths. I must learn to see them as God sees them, not as flesh and blood, but as soul and spirit.

I must learn to judge them with grace and mercy as I hope they will judge me. I must realize that the things they do are a result of the spirit that fills their lives. For all of us, the greatest need is to meet the one who is Master of all. Jesus willingly endured an agonizing torturous death at the hands of demon filled sinners, who were acting out all the hatred Satan possesses.

Yet Jesus was able to say from the cross they nailed Him to, ".....Father, forgive them, for they know not what they do." (Luke 23:34 NKJV) He rightly recognized the source of the evil and hatred they poured out on Him that day. And then His last words from the cross, "Father into your hands I commit My Spirit." (Luke 23:46 NKJV) Jesus knew the life force within Him was the spirit of God and the rightful home of the Spirit was in the presence of the Father. This truth should bring an abundance of peace and security to everyone who walks in the Spirit of God. During the brief moment in time, when my heart could not beat, I learned a little about the peace the Word of God tells us about. I could never adequately describe it! The best description I could give would be as if I had returned to the safety of my mother's womb. It was warm and secure, a place we all long for.

Chapter Four

Miracle Four, Divine Order in the Midst of Chaos

"He was literally delivered from the prison straight into the palace, ironically because the king had forgotten the dream. Remembering the dream was his salvation.

Photo Taken: Beautiful Blarney Castle, County Cork, Ireland. Used by permission.

Living the Dream

The man sat in the window of the lush palace provided to him by the king of the land. He was thinking about his life. He could not help but chuckle as he mused over the many events that brought him to this place. He never imagined the possibility he could end up the second in command to the king of the most powerful nation on earth. Never the less, here he was. After many years and much heartache, he was once again beginning to remember the dream!

His mind drifted back to the very early days of his life because today had been a very special day of reunion. He had been reunited with his brothers. They were a part of his family that he feared he would never see again. He thought first about his Father and the relationship they shared so long ago. Indeed, he had been the apple of his father's eye. It had now been several years since he had last seen him. His dream had separated them!

His mind carried him back through the many happenings, occurring during the past few years, since he last saw his father. He thought of all of the hardships he had faced, the disappointments, the fears and tragedies that he thought could never be erased. They now seemed but small things. He was now realizing the fulfillment of his faith. For the first time since early in his childhood, the revelations he had witnessed were coming to fruition. The things set adrift in his mind were now becoming a crystal clear reality. He was being carried by his dream!

God was revealing to him the purpose for his life. His heart had been torn from his chest as he experienced the betrayal of his brothers so long ago. Their envy had turned to hatred. How could they have rejected him, separating him from his father? Yet they did! He thought about betrayal and false accusations that had landed him in prison a few years earlier. He thought about his longing as time passed in the prison and no one remembered him. He was in a strange land forgotten and all alone. The dream for now seemed much more like a nightmare!

His reward for his faithfulness seemed to be ever fleeting from him. He remembers thinking, how could anything good possibly come from all of this? The reality of the dream deep inside him gave him assurance there was a divine plan for his life and in time he would know it. He continued on. He had a superior spirit that eventually gained him favor with the king. He was literally delivered from the prison straight into the palace. Ironically, this was because the king had forgotten his own dream. Remembering the king's dream was his salvation.

Through it all, he maintained his integrity and faithfulness. In large part, his dream had driven him to keep looking for God in all of his trials. As he looked, he always found exactly the thing he needed. It was divinely provided to him. So it is with our lives, though it may not come in a night vision as it did with Joseph. God has a dream for us all. If we stay faithful, every step we take will lead us to the fulfilling of that dream. We must keep living the dream because God is faithful.

As human beings, we all go to great efforts to make our lives as comfortable and orderly as we possibly can. But sometimes, caution loses out and crisis comes. It catches us unprepared and unaware, bringing chaos into our lives. This is true especially in the medical field when dealing with unique individuals who may respond well, or not so well, to the treatments they receive. In my case, what seemed to be a great recovery process was abruptly interrupted by an unforeseen issue. This abrupt issue changed all of our plans. None of us enjoy these kinds of surprises. However, we must remember that they happen for a reason.

Social Media-Legacy of Prayer and Faith:

Posted by: Beverly Rollins Dunn – Sept. 11ᵗʰ, 2013 Chattanooga Tn.

Tony has had a good but tiring day. We found out the test they ran on him for HIT, proved to be positive for a Heparin allergy that caused platelets to be destroyed. One of our prayer needs, at this time, is to have a decrease in liver enzymes that were found to be elevated this morning. Having a Heparin allergy puts him at a disadvantage for blood thinning. The newer blood thinner they started him on could not be given until creatinine was down and now can't be used because liver enzymes are elevated. We are on a newer med drip now. He is also having trouble with elevated blood pressures now and they need to stabilize. Please remember these things when you pray. Praises and honor to our good God! Thank you all!

Whether we choose to acknowledge it or not, there is a divine purpose and message in everything we face in life. God works through pain, discomfort, and trials just as much as He works through blessings and fellowship. Rest assured, whatever it takes for Him to get our attention….. He is willing to do. Sometimes, God's actions involve pain, because we have left Him no other choice. He understands that pain will get our attention in much the same way a good parent understands that a spanking will most likely get a child's attention. This truth comes contrary to the political correctness doctrine prevalent in our society in this modern age. However, the discipline of a good parent or a great God is indispensable in bringing about a blessed life.

In the following passages and commentary, I would love to explain to you what God has been telling me throughout this entire spirit altering ordeal. I do so because there is a very urgent need for all of us to sharpen our spiritual eyes and ears, especially those who seek after an active relationship with God. We need to tune into the very important things He is trying to tell us about our lives and how we are choosing to live them.

I am not sure Christians today understand the wickedness of the times we live in. I believe if we did understand, we would be living with a much greater sense of urgency. We would be attempting to be the watchman on the wall who warns an unsuspecting and ignorant world of all the impending dangers we are facing. Indeed, these are perilous times we are living in! I think God is choosing to reveal His power to us in ways we have never known in order to show His sovereign authority over this world and our lives. I feel deeply blessed that our all-powerful God has chosen to show His power to me, my family, and my friends. He has touched many others who have been eye witnesses to my case. Please allow me to try to share with you a scriptural explanation of some of the messages that I believe God has been delivering through it all.

A Message for Me, From Jonah and Jesus

(Matt 12:38 NKJV) Then some of the scribes and Pharisees answered, saying, "Teacher, we want to see a sign from You." 39 But He answered and said to them, "An evil and adulterous generation seeks after a sign, and no sign will be given to it except the sign of the prophet Jonah. 40 For as Jonah was three days and three nights in the belly of the great fish, so will the Son of Man be three days and three nights in the heart of the earth. 41 The men of Nineveh will rise up in the judgment with this generation and condemn it, because they repented at the preaching of Jonah; and indeed a greater than Jonah is here.

It is amazing how God can take many of the object lessons of scripture and bring them a person's memory, in a real life kind of way, and at the perfect time. After the trauma and miraculous visitations occurring during our hospital stay, I was left with a burning desire to know exactly what had happened. More importantly to me is why it had happened? Most of us as Christians and children of God understand that nothing happening to us in life is without meaning or purpose. God speaks through varied methods and means and all in the power of the spirit. It is up to us if we will eventually hear what it is he is saying. We must be attuned to His Spirit. As I began the healing process, the previous scripture was the first one that burned in my memory and began speaking to me. It bears a significant parallel message to the events that took place.

In addressing the questions of the religious leaders, Jesus drew from the truths of the little book of Jonah in the Old Testament. The book is the story of the calling and sending of Jonah into a wicked city to preach a warning from God to repent or perish. After a period of rebellion, Jonah delivered his message and the people repented and were spared.

In this New Testament passage, the wicked leaders of Jesus' day demanded a sign from Him in order to prove who Jesus really was. Instead, Jesus affirmed the simplicity and power of the ministry and message of Jonah. He compared Jonah's message to His own. As Jonah was three days and nights in the belly of the fish, so would Jesus be three days and three nights in the heart of the earth. Jesus made it clear to them He owed them no proof but that of His message, which was to repent or face judgment, just as Jonah's had been.

In doing this, Jesus offended their self-righteous attitudes. Jesus declared that the wicked men of Nineveh would rise up in judgment against the religious leaders of His day. The wicked men of Nineveh heard Jonah's message and repented. While the religious leaders heard Jesus' message, who is a greater one than Jonah, and would not repent. The hardest people to reach with the truth are those who think they already know the truth…..they are deceived. Unfortunately, this is a description of many of our religious Christian leaders and their followers today. The thing that spoke to me in Jonah's story was not the results of his message, but it was his response after he received the calling to go preach this significant message to Nineveh.

First of all, Jonah was reluctant to accept this call. Instead he can be found getting on a ship heading in the opposite direction from where God was leading him. To make matters worse, Jonah went down into the ship and fell asleep. Meanwhile, God sent a powerful storm to begin the process of getting Jonah back on the correct course. As Jonah slept, the ship's crew was battling the fury of the storm because of Jonah's disobedience. They were left to battle the ferocious storm in order to preserve their lives and those of their passengers.

Finally, when Jonah awakes he sees the hand of God in the storm and he hears the message. He understood that the storm was brought about as a direct result of his rebelliousness. Finally, in an act of submission, Jonah asked the crew to throw him overboard…..they reluctantly yielded. This act resulted in their immediate relief from the storm. These seasoned sailors were no match for the storm! In truth, no amount of knowledge or skill is sufficient when we use it to fight against the divine will of the Creator. Human effort will fall short every time.

This is the first truth I was able to apply to my experience concerning the day my heart stopped and the code blue was initiated. The medical team who responded to the call was highly skilled and capable. Even so, after fifty-five minutes with no response and no sign of recovery, they were ready to give up. The attending physician was preparing to make a pronouncement of death. I have been told that my heart beat then returned. It was as if God was saying, "Not until I say so!" To those attending the code, I became the "Miracle Man", a title they still use when I get the chance to visit. The real miracle however was the fact that God had orchestrated these events to bring about His purpose.

One of the first things I remember, after being taken off the respirator and weaned from some of the sedatives, was Dr. Portera coming into the room and speaking to me. He put his hand on my arm and said, "You are one strong man!" I did not know exactly what had happened to lead him to say that. My only thought was that it was not me who was strong, but God. My response to him was to point my finger upward. At that moment, I knew it was not my strength keeping me here…..it was Gods! I had never felt weaker than I did at that moment.

I have listened as my family and many of the doctors and nurses have described the event to me. It was day ten after surgery and I was scheduled to go home. My recovery had gone very well and we were all looking forward to home and healing. I got out of bed to go to the bathroom. As I came from the bathroom, I started having difficulty breathing. I sat in the bedside chair and told Beverly what I was experiencing. She immediately called for help, because she already knew. We had been waiting for Deanna, Dr. Portera's nurse, to come and make the discharge official. Deanna had been called to an unplanned meeting that morning.

We realized later that Deanna's "unplanned" meeting was a divine intervention. It was during this time that my lungs began to close up as the result of the formation of a "saddle clot" across both lungs. My divinely appointed storm was beginning, and Bev was mustering the crew that would be fighting to save me. If I had been released at the scheduled time that morning, the entire ordeal would likely have ended much differently. I would have been in the car heading home. My home is forty-five minutes away from the hospital.

I cannot say enough good things about the nurses on the fifth floor where this ordeal began that day. The quick response by the staff of the fifth floor, my nurse that day, Mariamma Varghese,RN, Holly Vandergriend,RN, and the fifth floor supervisor, Brook Kelly,RN, just to name a few, was part of the collection of angels that day for my divine intervention. I am told that within a few minutes they had me to the scan room where they confirmed I indeed had a saddle clot. I was then transferred to the MICU at the insistence of this fifth floor staff. I was to be treated for this clot and stabilized. Unfortunately, this clot proved to be more than the average medications could effect. I was in desperate need of a treatment called TPA. TPA is usually administered in another section of the hospital. There was nothing "usual" about my situation. I was too unstable to be moved from the MICU.

Dr. Steciw was in charge of the "code blue." The call was made for the TPA to be given in the MICU. There was no other choice. As I understand it, this treatment was not commonly performed in the MICU setting. When the TPA was finally administered to me, it caused my heart to completely stop.....for fifty-five minutes. More than three crash carts of medications and multiple procedure trays were used in my resuscitation. According to Dr. Portera, the exact number is uncertain. Three nurses took turns doing chest compressions. I am told I took the equivalent of fifty-five hundred hits to the chest during that time period. I remember being asked days later if my chest was sore, and amazingly, it was not and never had been.

The medical staff did all they reasonably could within their power and expertise to revive me and return normal function to my body. In the end, they had come to the place where they had done all that was humanly possible to do. By all appearances, I was gone and all their efforts would not change the outcome. Later when we did a follow-up visit to Dr. Portera, he admitted to us that he had concluded in his mind, as he watched the code blue team work, I was a dead man. He did not expect a recovery.

Interestingly, Dr. Portera would not tell them to stop the code when he was asked if they should "call it." As the sailors in the book of Jonah came to a place where they realized they were powerless against the storm, so did those who were battling my storm for me on this day. It was not until they were ready to surrender and cease their efforts that they saw the deliverance of the Lord. As the doctor was concluding the worst and was preparing to pronounce my death, my heart rate returned.

Bev and my son Justin had been allowed to come into the room near the middle of the code. She told me my eyes were opened, fixed, and glazed over. In her mind.....I was dead! That fact did not prevent her from whispering in my ear, requesting me not to leave. Justin stood in the doorway praying. He then moved to the foot of the bed but never ceased praying. Praying continued even after they returned to the waiting room. Many others, either there at the hospital or in their homes and places of work, were also praying at that very moment. I thank God for social media. Through it, prayer request spread rapidly that day.

Social Media-Legacy of Prayer and Faith:

Posted by: Tara Karis Oakes– Sept. 12ᵗʰ, 2013

Several people have asked for an update on Daddy, so here you go..... ☺

The miraculous recovery continues! The past six days have all emerged into one continuous strand of ups and downs, so I'm having difficulty organizing my thoughts. Lon-story-short: God has been faithful to answer the prayers of His people over and over and over again. Each specific need we have brought before the throne has been answered more quickly than – even with the most steadfast faith – we could have anticipated. All of Dad's systems/organs are functioning at or nearly functioning at 100 % & each concern that has arisen has either been resolved or is in the resolution process. God is so good!! I am overwhelmed by the unending support we have received during this time – the prayers, visits, encouragements, hugs, food, etc.

My prayer is that each of you – who have been so steadfast in your support for our family – are blessed beyond measure for your faithfulness and that God will continue to be glorified and lives changed through our testimonies.
Specific prayer still needed for.....

- **The new meds to continue stabilizing Dad's blood pressure and eliminating any remaining clots.**
- **Divine rest, peace and comfort, especially as he begins remembering/learning of the past few days events.**
- **Total healing of all systems with no setbacks.**

Love You all!!! ☺

I believe these prayers became the source of sustaining power that served to revive me and to protect me. There was a deliverance from long term damage, normally caused to the body, by such a traumatic event. It would be days of tests and diagnosis before all of my body functions were returned to normal. Always at the critical time, there would be another positive development and vital needs would be met.

Bev described the scene in the waiting room as Dr. Portera came in the last time to give an update on me. In her words, "He came in and sat down with a really blank look on his face and said, we have hope, his heart beat has returned." He described his concern that I would be brain damaged. He had performed a "sternal rub" test where you rub the center of the chest with the knuckles. It is a procedure that is quite uncomfortable to the one receiving. If a person is brain damaged, they will respond a certain way, a reflex. If the brain is intact, the person will attempt to resist, or respond in discomfort. To his surprise, I responded with discomfort. In disbelief, he repeated this procedure three times, and three times I responded with discomfort. Needless to say, he was both surprised and hopeful. For the following five days, I would be sedated and on a respirator until it could be determined all was clear.

My memory of the days immediately following the code are somewhat sketchy to say the least. I have been told of some of the unique things that happened as I was slowly being brought back to the land of the living. I remember waking up and seeing my family in the room. I remember feeling the pain of my rings cutting into my fingers because my hands were so swollen. I had asked for my rings after the surgery. They are very precious to me. My wedding band is a reminder of Bev and my family and the love we share. My faith ring, on my other hand, was a gift Bev gave me for my fiftieth birthday. This ring has the Star of David (Magen David) and is overlaid with the Cross of Christ. It is a visual reminder of my relationship with God and the Christian's bond with the Jewish people.

This day, I could feel the pain of the rings and wanted to have them removed. So, as best I could, I raised my hand and gestured as though I was writing something in the air. I was still intubated and could not speak and was wearing the special mitts preventing me from pulling out my tube. I remember my daughter Tara immediately saying, "He wants to write something!" The nurse gave Tara a pen and paper and to the nurses surprise I was able to write perfectly, "Rings". Bev told me later that they had asked me if I knew what had happened to me. I wrote perfectly, "Pulmonary Embolism." I do not have a clue how I possibly knew that and I am more impressed that I could spell it correctly. That is a miracle in itself.

Looking back, as God speaks to my heart about this message He has delivered to me, I understand a little better His purpose in this. I too have been asked to deliver a message and I have been reluctant to deliver it. The message He has ordained me to deliver is not one directed primarily at the lost world. It is one directed primarily at the one entity that can change a lost world and bring true deliverance to it. The Church is my God appointed mission field and battleground. The message I have been given is not one that will be readily embraced, at least not by many in church leadership. It is a message of indictment. It is the blistering message the prophets delivered to a backslidden Israel. The church in America, for the most part, is no longer the Church Jesus ordained. Religious formality and programming is reducing the Church to a social club or just another not-for-profit organization having its pastors as CEO's. This is a tragic evil.

What was meant to go forth in simplicity and power has been stifled. It has been made complicated and exclusive by wicked men and women who see themselves as guardians to their particular belief system. They are constantly dividing the body to create some new strain of faith they can then lord over. The Christian faith has been diluted by many who are luke-warm and spiritually ignorant believers. Many want to stay close enough to Christ to avoid hell and maintain the hope of eternity, while resisting the commitment of their whole lives in faith. We realize that true commitment will result in a change of behavior and appetite. These are two things we are not quite willing to give up. We have taken the blessed message of the scripture and crammed it into our tiny little religious box, over which we maintain meticulous control. We leave God nothing but our leftovers.

There is only one truth and it is God's Word in context. The multiple religious systems we find ourselves participating in, or in competition with, are the creation of humanity and only serve to divide the body of Christ. This has weakened what should be the most powerful spiritual force on earth. This is truly the spiritual dilemma that is enabling Satan to ransack and demoralize the American believer while reducing the Christian population to an insignificant and despised people. Jesus said it best, "A house divided against itself cannot stand." News flash: Satan realizes this too, and he is extremely proficient at division! We see the evidence more clearly all the time in the politics of our nation which has been highly influenced and enabled by the division in our churches.

There is a solution. Through humility and repentance the Church still holds the key to America's and the world's future. We have not been left here to prevent the coming and certain judgment of God. We have been left here to resist the advances of Satan. Our purposes are to prevent him from bringing more and more of humanity under his captivity and control, resulting in souls lost forever. As Abraham interceded for Lot in Sodom and Gomorrah, we too should be interceding on behalf of this perverted world in which we find ourselves living. Who knows, judgment may be stayed a few more hours by a Christian people who are willing to repent and seek the face of God in true relationship in these perilous times. We must commit ourselves to His dream for us!

My Faith and Me

(Acts 12:5—7 NKJV) Peter was therefore kept in prison, but constant prayer was offered to God for him by the church. 6 And when Herod was about to bring him out, that night Peter was sleeping, bound with two chains between two soldiers; and the guards before the door were keeping the prison. 7 Now behold, an angel of the Lord stood by him, and a light shone in the prison; and he struck Peter on the side and raised him up, saying, "Arise quickly!" And his chains fell off his hands.

And then a few verses later..........

(Acts 12:15—16) But they said to her, "You are beside yourself!" Yet she kept insisting that it was so. So they said, "It is his angel." 16 Now Peter continued knocking; and when they opened the door and saw him, they were astonished.

I chose the scripture above because I believe it is chocked full of great examples of my faith failures up until this point in my life. In fact, it outlines a great parallel of how we all waver and many times continue living out our faith in a purely superficial kind of way. In essence, we have no real expectations of any supernatural benefits of our faith at all. This particular scripture contains four main characters. These characters include Peter, the guards, the lady in the prayer meeting, and the leaders in the church. Its message provides us with the keys that point us to repentance and ultimately a return to Godly power and influence in the world.

**In fact, because of his fervent faith, Peter
found himself public enemy number one to
the Jewish religious leaders and then to Rome.
This set the stage for his arrest and ultimately
His divinely appointed encounter with God.**

**Photo of: Beautiful Blarney Castle Gardens,
County Cork, Ireland. Used by permission.**

First of all, we should look at the situation Peter found himself dealing with. We all know Peter was the disciple that had a tendency to be a little brash, outspoken, and a little worldly in his actions. At least the soldier who temporarily lost his ear at the arrest of Jesus might think so. We should remember however, it was Peter who was willing to step out of the boat onto the water that stormy night and attempt to walk the waves to Jesus. No one else volunteered.

Eventually, Peter went through a radical transformation. This happened specifically when he faced his failures of faith during the time of the trial and crucifixion of Christ. In fact, because of his fervent faith Peter found himself public enemy number one to the Jewish religious leaders and eventually to Rome. This set the stage for his arrest and ultimately a divinely appointed encounter with God.

As Peter slept in the prison cell that night, under guard and chains, I am sure his mind was filled with many doubts as to where this would all lead (As it was with Jonah, I am beginning to see a pattern here. God can accomplish great things even while we sleep.) He was very much a captive. He was chained to two guards on either side and at least two other guards kept watch at the prison gates. Satan was sure he had him.

Then something unexpected happened. There was a great light appearing only to Peter. The visitor woke no one else and did not gain any reaction from the guards. Then Peter saw the source of the light, an angel, who struck him on the side. He was then instructed to, "Arise quickly," as his chains fell off. Peter was uncertain. He did not know whether this was real or a dream. This is always the case when God is moving in a marvelous and supernatural way. Peter arose and walked out of the prison a free man. I have often wondered how the guards explained this to their bosses the next day.

Peter then makes his way to a place of safety. He goes to a place where he knows people love him and are praying for him. When he arrives he knocks at the door and is greeted by a woman. Apparently, the woman was so shocked at his appearance she forgot to let him in. Instead, she went back inside and told the others Peter was at the door, while all the time Peter stood knocking. The response of the others in the church was not quite what one may expect. Though they had been praying fervently for this very thing, apparently they did not believe it could really happen. They were totally unprepared to experience God's delivering power.

Their response was one of disbelief. In fact, it was easier for them to believe it was Peter's angel from the Lord than to believe that God actually had the power to liberate Peter from his prison cell and the guards who kept it. Is this disbelief a truth that stifles many Christian's faith today? The forces of the world seem too powerful to us! We retreat into this spiritual fantasy land with no expectation that God can radically impact our world in a purely physical way if He so chooses. Eventually, they opened the door for Peter and they were "Astonished!" It was actually him.

I ponder and absorb the truths of this passage, I cannot help but re-live the lessons I have learned as a result of God's intervention in my own life. For me, my captivity began to take form from the day I first learned of the cancer in my pancreas. It culminated in the day when my heart stopped and the code began. It has continued through the days that I have watched the healing process taking place. In the beginning, I wanted to believe God could and would intervene in a miraculous way to bring healing and restoration back to my life. But honestly, I would never have expected Him to do what He did. My limited faith would not allow me to go that far.

Social Media-Legacy of Prayer and Faith:

Posted by: Beverly Rollins Dunn – Sept. 12th, 2013 Chattanooga Tn.

> Tony is really good this morning but is ready to be back at our home in the valley.....the last of his allergy tests came back to reinforce that he is not only allergic to Heparin, he is "highly" allergic. Starting him on Coumadin today. Gonna sit him up.....he has not been OOB for six days. Liver enzymes are coming down and kidneys are fine and no heart damage.....all praise to God. He has given the doctors and nurses such gifts in aiding Tony's healing, from the beginning at Skyridge Medical Center to Memorial. Continue to thank you all, our family and friends for your support for holding the line for us in prayer.

I say this to my shame! I had a superficial kind of faith. I thought it in my head, but I did not really fully believe it in my heart. All of that has changed now! "God, forgive me for putting religious limitations and misinterpretations on your will as well as the divine working of your power." The day of the crash you showed up at my prison door and you commanded me to rise and made the chains of death fall off. Death had its grip on me and no authority on earth could stay its hand, but you! One day Jesus made a proclamation, "Therefore if the Son makes you free, you shall be free indeed"! (John 8:36 NKJV) absolutely, positively, free! He alone has the power! I know this first hand and will never doubt it again!

Spiritual Courage

There are many believers who have dedicated themselves to God and His purposes but have never surrendered wholly to those purposes. The quality of our relationship to God is not determined by what we choose to do for Him. It is determined by what He chooses for us and whether or not we are going to be obedient to do it. This is a truth I have struggled with for much of my adult Christian life. It is a truth many others struggle with, or in the very least, they need to be reminded so they can begin their struggle.

We must eventually come to the place where we can honestly submit our own wills to God and replace them with His will for us. I am so charged up when I have the opportunity to be around another believer who has a firm grasp of this principle. What is the benefit of calling ourselves Christians if we are not experiencing the life changing power that the message and presence of Christ brings to us? In the end, we have no excuse for not fully knowing the power and presence of God.

Spiritual Submission

> James 4:7 NKJV Therefore submit to God. Resist the devil and he will flee from you. 8 Draw near to God and He will draw near to you. Cleanse your hands, you sinners; and purify your hearts, you double-minded. 9 Lament and mourn and weep! Let your laughter be turned to mourning and your joy to gloom. 10 Humble yourselves in the sight of the Lord, and He will lift you up.

There is a huge laundry list of mistakes that I have made through the years that are more than enough evidence to prove my imperfections. It remains a mystery to me why God cares about me when I consider all the ways I have failed Him throughout my lifetime. There is at least one thing of which I am aware that I know I have done correctly. I believe it has made all the difference as he has visited me throughout this episode of my life.

That one right thing I have done is surrender. I remember the day when I bowed before Him and turned it all over to Him. I was broken and I knew beyond a shadow of a doubt that I needed Him. When I surrendered my will to Him, I meant it. I believe He took me at my word. When He accepted my commitment, I ceased to live a life on my own and began learning to live life as He directed. It was not my life to live anymore. I am living His dream, not my own! However, this does not mean I have not allowed myself to drift from the course many times, for regrettably I have. I am convinced that for as long as we remain in this earthly existence there will remain a constant battle between the temporal and the divine. Victory is as easy as committing the battle to the Lord. The only thing that is required of us is submission, devoid of selfish rebellion. God can fully handle the rest.

The promise of the scripture above says all that needs saying about what the relationship between a man and God should look like. There are a few things that are absolutely necessary if a person is to ever have an intimate relationship with his or her Maker. The first thing God expects is that His child will want to live near to Him in close fellowship. Doing this requires a hunger and thirst for God's Word. His Word is a verbal picture of who He is, what He loves, and what He hates.

To make it perfectly clear there are things God hates! These are things He wants and expects us to hate as well. This is a statement that contradicts political correctness. This is why we are accused of hate speech so often when we talk about sin. It remains true however, God hates sin and we should too. God expects His people to hate the same things He hates and to tell the world about it without apology but, not with self-righteous proclamations. Instead, we should share this message with humility, love, and spiritual authority and power. Pleasing Him involves accepting and applying His Word in its purity. This application must begin with our own lives before we attempt to engage the enemy. We must remember that the enemy is not those who want to disagree and argue. The enemy is the deceptive spirits who possess those who refuse the truth.

God takes great pleasure in watching a human being defeat Satan by using the weapons He has provided. One should read the book of Job for this example. God will then watch as we submit and humble ourselves under the power of His wings, giving Him glory for it all. I believe of all the acts that we can perform, humanly speaking, to humble ourselves in submission is by far the most powerful one. It is through our humility that

He imparts the trust and the skill to handle His spiritual weaponry and wield it effectively.

Authentic Faith

(John 11:40 NKJV) Jesus said to her, "Did I not say to you that if you would believe you would see the glory of God?"41 Then they took away the stone from the place where the dead man was lying. And Jesus lifted up His eyes and said, "Father, I thank You that You have heard Me. 42 And I know that You always hear Me, but because of the people who are standing by I said this, that they may believe that You sent Me." 43 Now when He had said these things, He cried with a loud voice, "Lazarus, come forth!" 44 And he who had died came out bound hand and foot with grave clothes, and his face was wrapped with a cloth. Jesus said to them, "Loose him, and let him go."

Some of my friends now lovingly address me as Lazarus and we get a chuckle out of it. At first, this made me uncomfortable. It is much farther out there than I have ever been willing to go. As I have studied and prayed about it, the Lord has helped me to understand more about how he used this incident in my life. He drew me back to the scripture concerning the raising of Lazarus. He helped me to understand what it was He was accomplishing the day he made His visit to Martha and Mary in Bethany. God also helped me to understand why He made His visit to Memorial Hospital on my behalf.

Social Media-Legacy of Prayer and Faith:

Posted by: Beverly Rollins Dunn – Sept. 13th, 2013 Chattanooga, Tn.

I have had many things to contemplate while living this miracle at the hospital with Tony. I'm so very thankful for the legacy of faith that my mom and dad, Roy and Katherine

Rollins, so wonderfully raised us in. I cannot even imagine the past few weeks without the love and grace of God, my Father, as taught to me by them. I love them dearly and have been blessed to have them standing in the gap for one grateful daughter.

Tony is great today, and has walked the hall in ICU. Eating full liquid diet and he has been released by the nephrology doctor.

First of all, He took me on a trip back to Genesis. I found the account where He created the first man from the dust of the earth. He breathed into his nostrils the breath of life and man became a living soul. There I stopped! As I mentioned earlier, I have always been reluctant to accept that a person could ever die, really die, and then be allowed to come back to life in their natural body. There are several instances which beg to differ in both the old and new testaments. I somehow bought into the doctrine of most contemporary religions effectively ruling out this possibility. I chose to believe God no longer worked in the same ways as He did then. Ironically, I held this belief as a result of scriptural interpretation or better stated….. Misinterpretation. The scripture does tell us it is appointed unto man once to die and then after this the judgment. My interpretation—a man cannot die and then return to life!

As I re-read Genesis, the Holy Spirit arrested me reminding me of something I had chosen to overlook. If God created a man from dirt and then breathed into him the breath of life, then who had the authority to say that He could not take away the breath of a man, already formed, then put it back if He so chooses? In fact, my son Justin blew me away when we gathered at his house for Thanksgiving in 2013, just days after my release from the hospital. We were sitting around talking with his father and mother in-law, Jerry and Norma Calaway, about what had happened the day of the code.

Justin shared with us the specific prayer he prayed during the time my heart had stopped. He petitioned God by stating, "God, you put Adam's breath in Him and I know you can return dads breath to him." Justin had no idea about the argument I was having with myself and with God, since having left the hospital. However, God was leading me to the same conclusion. I had no idea that he had prayed that prayer. I guess the question remaining is this…..why would God choose to do such a thing? I found the answer in the story of Lazarus. (John 11:1-33 NKJV)

Jesus gave two reasons for raising Lazarus from the grave. The first reason was so that those who believe would see the glory of God. The second reason was so that those who did not believe would come to believe that He (Jesus) had been sent by Almighty God. In other words, as verification that Jesus was indeed who He said He was and could exercise in the power and authority of the Creator Himself. Here we must accept the fact that the Father did not withhold any of His power from the Son. I think both of these reasons require some amount of explanation because it is so easy to misconstrue the message. This is something I have been a victim to my entire Christian life.

When a person first becomes a Christian, they do so as an imperfect human being who is in need of experiencing the perfect and divine presence of God in their lives. From the moment we first believe in Christ our lives will begin to change. Our challenge is to go forth into life surrendering our own wills, desires, and unbelief as they arise, in exchange for the will of our Savior. This is no easy task! In this sense, our salvation or deliverance takes place throughout our lifetime.

> I believe this truth is reflected in the following scripture which enlightens us. (Phil 2:12 NKJV) "Therefore, my beloved, as you have always obeyed, not as in my presence only, but now much more in my absence, work out your own salvation with fear and trembling; 13 for it is God who works in you both to will and to do for His good pleasure."

Social Media-Legacy of Prayer and Faith:

Posted by: Suzan Carson Bynum – Sept. 14th, 2013

Meet my friend Tony Dunn, 8 days ago he survived a code lasting more than 30 minutes, he has no brain injury from throwing blood clots to both lungs, his kidneys are functioning normally, and the labs are stable, he is back on

full liquids again and Bev says he wants to go home to their house in the valley......AMEN I SAY AND AGAIN I SAY AMEN AND THANK YOU TO OUR HEAVENLY FATHER

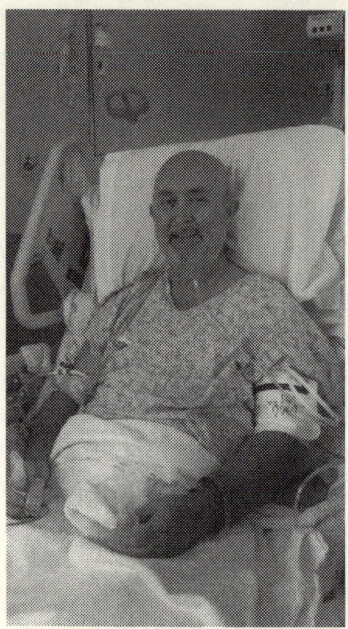

A Very Thankful "Me", After the Code!

We are not told to try to do it our own way. The only way is "through Christ" who we have made Lord of our lives. Instead, we are told to deal with the sins in our lives using the power of Christ, through the Holy Spirit, as He reveals our sins to us. We had no idea of the sin that was hiding within us when we first became a Christian. We did not know what God was going to do in order to deliver us of that sin. We would have been petrified and scared to death had we known. Stealth is sins greatest weapon forged against us! Jesus visited the home town of Lazarus and the believers there had no idea what God was about to do. His actions would strengthen their faith and purge them of their hidden unbelief.

This divine appointment was one leaving those believers there in amazement. The immediate need in their lives was to see the "Glory of God", as Jesus stated when He lifted His voice in prayer. His action speaks volumes about God's willingness to reward His sometimes struggling children. He visits them with a divine display of spiritual power in order to blow away their doubts, fears, and defeats. God knew these believers were heartbroken and in deep despair at the loss of their brother and friend. Jesus himself felt their despair. It was at this scene we read the shortest verse in the Bible, "Jesus wept!" (John 11:35 NKJV)

The second reason was for Christ to touch those who had not yet believed that He was who He said He was. Jesus prayed to the Father, "that they may believe You sent me." I have heard it asked many times, "Why did Jesus perform the many miracles that He performed during His earthly ministry?" In truth, with our limited understanding, we cannot possibly know what was in the mind of Christ or why He did the things He did. In this case, He specifically tells us.

In general, I believe most of the acts of Jesus were performed in the spirit of revelation. These acts were to reveal His power over all the things that hold humanity captive. These were things such as disease, evil, spiritual bondage, religious deception, and demonic possession as well as death itself. All of these things came under His authority. These are things that humanity is subject to in the course of living and have very little power in themselves to prevent. More than revelation, I believe compassion for our infirmities was His greatest motivator. Jesus could not prevent Himself from doing the things He did. He loved us way too much. He realized full well that these acts of power were setting Him on a collision course with the religious powers, the temple priest, and would eventually cost Him his mortal life. This was the cross He bore long before He had to bear the cross.

As I write these words today, I do so with a new sense of humility and submission. I have been to the throne of grace to beg forgiveness for my unbelief and arrogance concerning the power of God and how He may or may not choose to display that power. I have invested more than thirty years in serious Bible study. I have scoured through hundreds of volumes of various commentary and I am left to admit that God has proven once again that, "Oh, the depth of the riches both of the wisdom and knowledge of God! How unsearchable are His judgments and His ways past finding out!" (Rom 11:33 NKJV)

At a time of His own choosing and for reasons beyond our ability to understand, God reveals deep, purposeful, and powerful things about Himself to His children and to the world for that matter. The greatest tragedy of all of modern Christianity is the way we have denigrated our God. We have subjected Him to our own, self-imposed, religious limitations. We have crammed this huge and boundless God into the tiny box of institutional theology. The term theology, "The study of God" is itself a gross oxymoron. For the scripture declares that His ways are passed finding out through mere study alone. Yet, for some reason we seem perfectly willing to send our young ministers to seminary to be schooled in God. We then turn the future of the church over to them as though they are somehow better prepared. We must begin emphasizing the calling of God on their lives. He will then send them to serve in the place of His choosing.

I believe God is as impressed with most seminary professors and alumni as He was with the temple leaders of Jesus day. These temple leaders He referred to as snakes and vipers, physicians with no value..... Professional religionist!! The church would be much more effective if the people would get on their knees and begin praying for the presence and power of the Holy Ghost. We must become willing to kick all the religious programming to the curb. Quit competing with each other for the tithe and start contending with the world for the sake of Godly truth and for the conversion of lost souls. This is what we should be about! It is certainly what God is all about!

In the final analysis, I can look back and thank God for it all. What seemed to be a chaotic and impossible situation, as the doctors and nurses worked frantically to save me that day, was in actuality a divinely planned and orchestrated event. Unbeknownst to us, the outcome had been pre-determined in heaven. We should all take heart that this is the case in the lives and trials of all believers. Chaos is only chaos to us! It is a word "never" spoken in heaven. I suppose realizing this is one reason why the apostle Paul was able to proclaim of his relationship to God, "Not that I speak in regard to need, for I have learned in whatever state I am, to be content:" (Phil 4:11 NKJV) Paul knew there was divine purpose in it all and more importantly he accepted that fact. So should we!

Chapter Five

Miracle Five, a Divine Visit, a Lifetime Reconciled

"As I look back, it still amazes me. It took God fifty five minutes to put my whole life-time into perspective by reconciling my past, validating my present, and redirecting my future. My understanding of God, even though He is passed fully understanding, has been eternally changed. I will never be the same, and will never see things the same again."

Photo of: Beautiful Blarney Castle Gardens, County Cork, Ireland. Used by permission.

As A Child............

I remember the early days of life and growing up in a small rural area. My thoughts never drifted too far from the simple life that I was living. I was a farm boy and was taught early in life to contribute through hard work and submission to the will of my dad. We were so young when we went to work on the farm. Dad would tie wooden blocks to our shoes so that our legs were long enough to reach the pedals on the tractor. He was a strict disciplinarian and would not put up with the things he considered nonsense or unimportant. There is always much to do on the farm and this was a constant reminder for us every day.

On each day of our summer break from school, my brother and I were met with a long list of tasks that were to be accomplished before dad arrived home from work. We were fully aware that there must be a serious effort to each one of those task. There must be evidence that we had tried to complete them even if we were incapable of accomplishing the task to dad's satisfaction. The alternative to not putting forth the effort was unacceptable, and dad was great at discerning whether or not we had put forth a serious effort. He had high expectations of our performance and was unyielding in our meeting all of those expectations. Excuses were never sufficient and totally unacceptable. In hindsight, many of the things we accomplished as young boys would be totally unimaginable for children in this modern age. While our friends were riding bikes, going to the swimming hole, and doing what most kids do with their free time on summer break, my brother and I were about the business of the farm.

Eventually, we began to see that our hard work did not go unnoticed. Dad began to reward us with horses, bikes, and even motorcycles. Of course this came with restrictions. Our use of these toys was contingent on our ability to continue to produce results on the farm. The toys had to be kept in their place and enjoyed only after the work was done. This restriction did not leave too many windows for folly. As we grew up, I remember how the environment began to change. My older brother became less and less tolerant of the farm life and of the constant pressure to produce.....as did I. This would result in an occasional outburst of anger and rebellion and sometimes a physical confrontation with dad. My brother Jeff, eventually joined the Navy and moved on to build his own life. I did not blame him. I admired him for his courage and for standing up for what he felt was right. This was a courage I did not possess. For me, it would not come until sometime much later. I would observe the sometimes heated disagreements between the two of them and vow to never go there. I remained silent.

My brother and I were both too young to understand that our dad was playing the role of all the hardships and tribulations that we would face throughout our lifetime. He was pushing us to face the ugliness that life can sometimes dish out. This was the conditioning for our future as we would move forward to start out own families and make decisions on how to deal with all the unexpected trials that would inevitably arise. Dad taught us to deal with hardship and adversity early on. In my opinion, things did not need to be as hard as he made them. But again, that is only my opinion (wink)! We did not realize it at the time, but it was a great gift.

I have come to appreciate dad's wisdom in a special way. It was a life medicine that tastes bad going down but produces great results. I believe that he taught us in the way that he did because he was young boy in the difficult years of the depression. He too left home at a very early age and became responsible and independent long before children are taught to be self-sufficient. Regardless of the reason, those early days were both a blessing and a curse for us. Those days were life in the raw. They were a reminder to enjoy the blessings when they come and then to hunker down when the trials arise, as they most surely will.

In hindsight, I love and appreciate my dad. He is still with us and he, as his father before him, has certainly been softened through the years. I believe he too had to reconcile the many trials he had faced along the way. I think he has learned to defeat many of the demons he struggled with throughout the years. It is hard for a child to finally reach the point where they can see their parent as an imperfect human being, just as they are themselves. Although I could never adopt the same extremes he used, at least to the same degree, I certainly understand what he was attempting to accomplish. It was noble. I see the results each day, and I thank God daily for this tough love that molded our resolve while leaving us with our own demons to conquer. But that too is life.....We are all responsible to conquer the demons plaguing and oppressing us—to blame someone else or make excuses is unacceptable.

Fortunately, we do not have to go it alone. Everything we need to learn about life and how to deal with it can be found in the Word of God. All the power we need to overcome those demons that have attached themselves to us can be found in the Holy Spirit. Our faith then becomes our power to overcome the obstacles that just seem too big for us. Deliverance will come in time!

My Mom and my sisters have also experienced their share of hardships and trials as they have struggled to reconcile those early years. Unfortunately for them, life was extremely difficult. The relationship that should exist between a husband and wife, and father and daughters, was strained at best throughout the early years. I did not realize, until much later in life, that dad was probably most influenced during his early years. Dad was witness to a "difficult" relationship between his father and mother. Later in life, he confided his experiences of lying in bed at night and hearing the activities taking place between his parents in the other room. He admitted it had gotten so bad that he and one of his brothers actually began talking of meting out their own justice on papaw, for grandma's sake. Even though Papaw eventually became saved and forgiven, the scars of the early days upon some of his children were very real. Those children turned out very well. I think I have some of the coolest relatives anywhere. They are a living breathing testament to the grace of God. It is the nature of sin to have long term consequences. I am sure papaw was just living out some of his own experiences.

Regardless of the source of this early influence, I believe it deeply affected the psyche of my dad. Although I think he was unaware of it at the time, this made it extremely difficult for him to understand and manage the relationships of his household. Again, as papaw before him, he lived out his experiences.

My mom is a saint of saints. Through her internal fortitude, she dealt with the many things that "by today's standards" would be considered emotional abuse. It was mom that really convinced me of the power of faith and trust in God. Most women in her position would have collapsed under the weight of it all. It was mom's faith that carried her through. Mom is my hero. She lived out the power even though I witnessed many times when she was pushed to the breaking point. She held strong.....thanks be to God. I know she will have a crown full of jewels when she reaches glory someday. I am thankful she is still with us.

In those early years, my older sisters also experienced their share of difficulties. In some ways, their difficulties were much greater than mine or my brother. They were expected to help take care of the details of our daily lives and many times without reward or recognition. Dealing with the difficulties of the day was very hard for them. Life was definitely harder in those days. Many of the lessons we all learned came through trial and difficulty. I do believe however that growing up in a home where expectations were high has served me and all my siblings well. It has helped us to accept responsibility and to take ownership in the challenges we face as adults. This is a powerful gift.

Fortunately for all of us, time has helped us to put things into perspective and the grace of God has saturated us with the ability to understand and forgive where necessary. We have come to understand many of these early hardships were a result of the scars that had been passed on for generations and into early childhood experiences. They were not deliberate as are most examples of such difficulties. I suppose there are many families who could share their own testimony of similar obstacles and hardships and some much worse. In the end, we are all responsible for how we deal with the trials and tragedies of our lives. We will never move on to overcome if we resort to holding a grudge, making excuses for wrong behavior, or blaming someone else. Failure to take ownership will only result in our refusal to see that there is no excusing surrender or failure.

Every person must come to the place in life where they put childhood experiences into perspective and overcome their scars. It matters little why they are there or by whom the injuries were caused. This is not a suggestion! It is a requirement if a person ever expects to live a life of victory over circumstances. The following passage of scripture is a power source that has helped me to rely on faith when the obstacles seem too big for me to handle on my own. It reminds me there will be things that seem too big to overcome. The demons we face in our lives will only be defeated by trusting God in faith. We cannot do it alone.

(Matt 17:19 NKJV) Then the disciples came to Jesus privately and said, "Why could we not cast it out?" 20

So Jesus said to them, "Because of your unbelief; for assuredly, I say to you, if you have faith as a mustard seed, you will say to this mountain, 'Move from here to there,' and it will move; and nothing will be impossible for you."

As a Young Man.........

Eventually, my days of rebellion would come forth as a flood and would be released upon my world with a satanic fury. I had become an angry young man and the years of pent up frustrations, along with other more current events, had finally pushed me to the breaking point. Although my anger was primarily a rebellion against my dad, the results would have an impact on many and especially my mom. I considered mom perfectly innocent. For six years, between the ages of fourteen and nineteen, I would partake of every vice I could. I would drink, smoke dope, pop pills, be sexually promiscuous, become a thief, and basically live a violent and reckless nomadic lifestyle.

As a result of my anger, my intentions in all of this became deviously simple. My motive was revenge. I understood these things would shame my dad because they were the things he taught us we should never do. I chose the friends that I knew he would disapprove of the most. I went to work illegally (relative to my young age) in a carpet mill and started living the life of a nomad. I would sometimes travel with a small group of older friends. There were times I would wake up alone, having thrown my sleeping bag down the night before on a rock pile, in the middle of some farmer's field. I would wake up in the morning to the sound of a truck idling as the farmer sat inside looking down at me shaking his head. Many times. I would walk until I was tired. I would find a spot somewhere beside a country road to sleep. Nothing mattered to me. I was driven by anger and there was no reaching me for a long period of time.

Fortunately for me, my sisters would eventually come to the rescue. I am not sure how long they had to search to find me, but I am sure glad they did. My older sister Deloris, offered me a room at her home and I accepted. Until very recently, I have not realized how much she helped me begin the healing process simply by offering unconditional love with no strings attached. And then Brenda, my next to oldest sister, offered me a place in her home.....again showing love with no strings attached. As I recall these times, I am filled with thankfulness for the love they have shown in rescuing me. I am not sure I have ever sufficiently said "Thank You" to them or have shown them my gratitude. This is something I must do!!

My sisters, Brenda Alford and Deloris Anderson

Eventually, the invitation came from home. Dad and mom offered me a place to stay. They had even prepared a room in the basement where I could barricade myself in.....again with no strings attached and no expectations. I accepted the offer although I continued to live my rowdy lifestyle for several more years. I am not sure how long, but many months elapsed before I ever ventured upstairs or sat down to a family meal with them. I do recall one specific incident when dad came into my room. This was something he would never do. I had been out the night before with my buddies. He had just gotten word that a warrant would be taken out on me for attempted murder. My buddies and I had gotten into a shootout with one of my friend's girlfriend's father the night before. Fortunately for me, the charges were dropped because I was a minor and after I made the promise to clean my life up.

After I had my fill of fights, car chases and car crashes, shootouts and bar room brawls, I began to understand what was really going on in my life. There were two very specific spiritual events that had occurred in my early years. These events would come back and revisit me at this particular time in my life. The first thing was the memory of happier days when I had first accepted Christ as my savior and made him Lord of my life. The second thing I remember was a very foolish prayer that I had prayed just before I deciding to allow anger to take control of my life. In reality, I had turned my life over to Satan. This fact was not clear to me at the time.

In a way, I had become the prodigal son who was finally coming to his senses. I am thankful that God is patient with His children. If not, He would have never honored that prayer. I prayed this prayer on a day when we were having a really nasty electrical storm in the area. I was angry and I remember going outside, in the wind and rain, and setting down cross legged in the yard. At this point in time, I knew God had the power to direct a lightning bolt to come down and fry me on the spot. In my mind, it was ok if he chose to do that. I prayed a simple but very foolish prayer and it went something like this, "God, if you will be patient with me, I want to find out if there is anything out there that is better than you! And if I find there is nothing better, I will serve you and do whatever you desire!"

Much later, when I started recollecting this prayer, it became clear to me how I had wasted so much time, and in essence, I was allowing anger to destroy me. I had not found anything better in all of my exploits. And then another revelation came…..it came in the most unlikely of places…..a beer joint. It was on a Friday evening and the party was in full force. Suddenly, a young man jumped up on the bar and began to preach. I mean country, back woods hacking and Bible-thumping kind of preaching. I did not know what to make of it until it became obvious that he was mocking his dad who was a preacher. I did not know this man in the bar and was unable to make any connection to him at the time. All I could feel was a cold shiver go up my spine. I remember thinking, "this guy has no idea what he is doing." Suddenly, I realized I had not lost my fear of God. It was still there.

I later found out that his dad was a preacher I had known earlier in my life. In the years before my rebellion, he was also a bus driver who had ushered our church choir back and forth to singing engagements. I loved this preacher. He had the sweet spirit of God on his life. I did not make the connection until the next day. My buddies pulled into the driveway and shared that this young man had been killed in a fiery car crash on his way home from the joint that very night. All I could think about was his sweet father, who was now very old. He would now be grieving over his wayward son as he was laid to rest. I did not want my life to end this way.

Needless to say, the party life lost its luster considerably that day. God turned His attention to me. God reminded me of the promise I had made in that simple prayer. That very day, I shared with my buddies what had really happened the night before at the beer joint and why it had happened. They had never really been exposed to God, His doctrine, and His law. I had not helped them to see, for I was in my years of backsliding. I confessed to them my rebellion and I begged them to forgive me and allow God to forgive them. I am not sure, but I believe they all eventually made professions of faith and two of the three have already passed on.....I hope to glory!

For good measure, soon after this experience, I began to have a recurring dream. In the dream, I was driving down the road and I noticed the clouds rolling in the distance. It was unlike a storm cloud. It was moving deliberately and quickly and ever expanding. It had brightness to it, unlike the dark clouds we are accustomed to seeing. Then as the cloud approaches, it continues to get brighter and brighter and as the brightness passes and it becomes clear. It is not a cloud at all. It is horses with riders, with swords drawn as though they are charging into battle, absolutely astounding and glorious to behold. The expression on their faces is that of anger. Their eyes are glaring with anger like fire and are locked onto their enemy. It is as though they see nothing else. The world does not even exist to them. They are detached from any human activity. The roar of their horses is unlike any noise I have ever heard. The only comparison I can make would be the loudest thunder clap I have ever heard, except sustained. It does not end until the horses are long out of sight. There is absolutely no doubt in my mind that this enemy is about to be absolutely and positively annihilated.

I have no doubt in the brightness, unseen to me, was the King of Kings. But they ride by me.....I miss it! I wake up in a cold sweat. I can only think that I do not want to miss this. I want to be "one" with them!

I realized that God had just allowed me to see a holy sight. I believe it is the saints and the angels with the King of Kings and Lord of Lords. How foolish it was for me to waste all of these years.

And then the final straw…..One day there is a knock at the door. It is a preacher! During the years of my rebellion, I had deliberately avoided preachers. I had not spoken to a single one through all of my escapades. But now, it is as though God is saying, "Ok son, and let us make this official!" So I did. As I write, I am setting here trying to remember who that preacher was…..and I cannot. It leaves me wondering…..was it really a preacher? Was it a man or an angel? I am really not sure. Maybe I will know someday. Most importantly that day, I rededicated my life to God and began the process of seeking His will in a new and very urgent way.

I had finally come to the place where I knew through experience, there is absolutely nothing better than the finished work of salvation through Jesus and the power of being called a son of God. God had taught me what I needed to know. He honored my foolish prayer. For the first time, I really began to experience God as Father. It was only at this revelation that I could begin to put things into perspective and really begin the reconciliation process with my own dad.

> (Ephesians 6:1—4 NKJV) Children, obey your parents in the Lord, for this is right. 2 "Honor your father and mother," which is the first commandment with promise: 3 "that it may be well with you and you may live long on the earth." 4 And you, fathers, do not provoke your children to wrath, but bring them up in the training and admonition of the Lord.

> (Proverbs 22:6 NKJV) Train up a child in the way he should go, and when he is old he will not depart from it.

As a Man, Becoming a Man of God………….

As I stepped into my new life, I did so with zeal and anticipation. I was driven by thankfulness that God had seen me through those darkest of days in my life. I would soon realize His plans were sure and His purpose was true. In hindsight, I can see how this new period of my life was the beginning of a purging and purifying of my life. It was the beginning of a period much like the forty years that Israel was sentenced to wander in the wilderness until the unfaithful generation had passed.

Fortunately, the dreams did not cease and God continued to guide me and inspire me through night visions. As I began this section of the book, one particular visitation has returned to me. Even though I thought I understood the message of it then, I have only come to realize the full significance of it now. In this dream, I believe God has outlined the course of these later years of my life and even to this very day and beyond. The memory of this revelation has helped me to understand why God has chosen to intervene in my life in a supernatural way.

This dream was unlike the other one, in that it occurred only once. It happened shortly after I was married and had started planning for the future to build my own family. The dream troubled my spirit for several days after it occurred. I could not interpret it! It was unlike the first dream in which I wake with a clear message. With this dream, I awoke very troubled. I had no idea what it meant, but I knew it was significant and contained a message. I was so troubled that there was a noticeable change in my behavior. After a few days had passed, my wife asked specifically what was bothering me. We talked about it and tried to make sense of it. Looking back, I believe the answer did begin to become clear, although broadly interpreted. The specific revelation did not become clear until now. Amazingly, this dream outlined the events and circumstances that would challenge my spiritual development to this very day. Let me explain.

In this dream, I found myself back at the old block structured farmhouse where I had spent most of my younger days. This house had a long driveway, of maybe 100 yards or more. I enjoyed watching as cars and people would come driving or walking by. In the dream, I am outside and I notice a very strange sight coming down the road. It has the appearance of a military regiment, except the soldiers are ordered from the front to back, smallest to largest. The unit appears to be shaped like a marching wedge, sharp point forward. As they approach the driveway, they turn and move toward our house.

I remember walking out onto the front yard to greet them, although I was uncertain exactly what I was greeting. As they approached, I noticed they had the same sort of countenance as the riders I had seen in the dream from my last days as a prodigal. Their expression however, was different. It was not righteous indignation as before. It was a scowling, putrid, and hatred. It was satanic. I could feel the coldness. It was a feeling that I had experienced on several different occasions during my days of rebellion. In fact, I was standing in almost the same place, where in real life, I had sat out in the thunder storm as an angry young man. I had no problem discerning this evil. They too marched passed me without giving me notice. When I turned, I realized they were all going into my house..... then it was quiet. In fact, they were quiet even as they marched. I never heard them.....perfect stealth.

Even though I knew this was not good, I felt compelled to go inside, so I did. As I viewed the intruders, I noticed they had all walked around the parameter of the room and had taken a seat. I noticed a being seated in the center of the group. I had not seen this being upon their entrance. It was as though he was already in the house when the others arrived. He was different, emotionless, cold, aloof, but beautifully clothed. One could tell he was the central authority figure. At this point, not one word had been uttered. Then, without a sound, he gazes at the smallest member of his entourage and I follow his gaze. And with a nod towards the smallest one, with no words uttered, the little fellow attacks me much like a mad dog would attack someone. I respond. It took little effort to defeat the little fellow and then he was gone. What ensued was beyond imagination. This same action was repeated to the next in line. The leader was going around the room. With every nod, the attacker was more vicious and more difficult. As the fights raged on, the interior of the house was being reduced to rubble.

Eventually, the fighting moved outdoors. Even though the captain did not come outside, he seemed to know when to send his next minion into the fray. As I fought, the wounds began to accumulate in my body. I was bleeding more and more and I could feel the strength gradually leaving me. In the back of my mind, I knew the worst was yet to come. The enemy would only become stronger and stronger, but I continued to fight and pray as I fought.

Then finally it happened, the being that initiated the battle came from the house. He had transformed into a beast more vicious than all those who came before. I have never known a fear like I felt in that moment as I faced this hideous creature. He held two swords…..one in each hand. I had no strength. I had no weapons. I was a bloody form of a man, totally spent. As I struggled with myself, trying to decide how to react, I stepped behind the house and hid beside the wall. I came to realize in that moment this was not my war to win. I prayed to God. "God, I cannot do this. I am weak. I have no more strength, but I am willing to try if it is your will." And then I received His response. His response was audible, simple, and clear. I have never forgotten what He said. I still hear it every time I find myself in a place of desperation or despair. He said, "Give me your best and I will do the rest!" At that point, I knew if God wanted me to win the battle then He would have to do it himself. It was much bigger than myself. With that, I mustered all the strength I could. I ran at the beast and launched my body into his, then all went dark.

As the light began to return, the scene before me left me awestruck and amazed. The first thing I noticed was this huge beast lying lifeless on the ground in front of me. I felt the force of two heavy objects lying against me, one on my right side and one on my left side. As I looked, it was the swords of the beast. They were bloody but not from my wielding. I tried to lift them. I could not lift even one of them with both hands. Until recently, I had not known weakness such as this. In the days immediately following my total body crash, I was reminded. The weakness I felt was not a dream. It was a coming reality. In this dream I describe now, thirty-five years ahead of time, God showed me He had intervened to conquer the enemy. I had willingly allowed this enemy to come into my life and my house, in my earlier rebellious years. He had exorcised an enemy who was reluctant to give up the place I had given them. He showed up again in the MICU at Memorial hospital to deny them their ultimate victory, my death!

I remember thinking about the shepherd boy who became King David and about the day he was to face Goliath, the huge champion of the godless Philistines. Saul gave David weapons he did not have the strength to wield, so he refused them, relying instead on His God to direct the stone from the sling to the desired place. And God did it! I realized for real that day, the battle is truly the Lords. As a man, I will never have enough strength in myself to defeat this enemy. None of us will!

There were other things I noticed as I stood there on the grounds that day. There were other beings who were busy cleaning up and carrying the remains of the fallen away. As I looked closer, I realized I had seen them before, except under different circumstances. It was the same riders I had observed in the first dream I described, the horsemen charging into battle. Now, they had a countenance of praise. The fire of vengeance no longer burned in their eyes. The battle had been won and victory secured, and yes, it was total annihilation. I realized, I did not miss it at all. God had actually fought for me! He allowed me to see His final victory.

As I shared with you the weakness I felt that day, in my first recollection this dream, it caused cold chills to run up my spine and brought tears to my eyes. For the first time, I realized the weakness and vulnerability I had felt during that dream. It was exactly the same weakness and vulnerability I had felt as I emerged from the code at the hospital. As I look back, it seems God was saying once again, "Give me your best, and I will do the rest!" He certainly did!

It was never my power that rescued me that day or any other day, but His! Through all my years, His purposes are unchanged. They have remained the same. He has never given up. He has been waiting for me to come home. How amazing are His ways and His faithfulness! In my weakest, He has always shown Himself most strong. I am so thankful He has been there with me through it all.

And now, for the first time in my adult life, I understand many of the things I thought I never would. I realize my life, even though it has been full of imperfections and trouble, has a purpose. The things I thought were curses have become blessings. I see His hand in the many trials that I could not understand before. He has been good to His Word. He has been there all along and guiding me with an unseen hand, just as He has for all of His children.

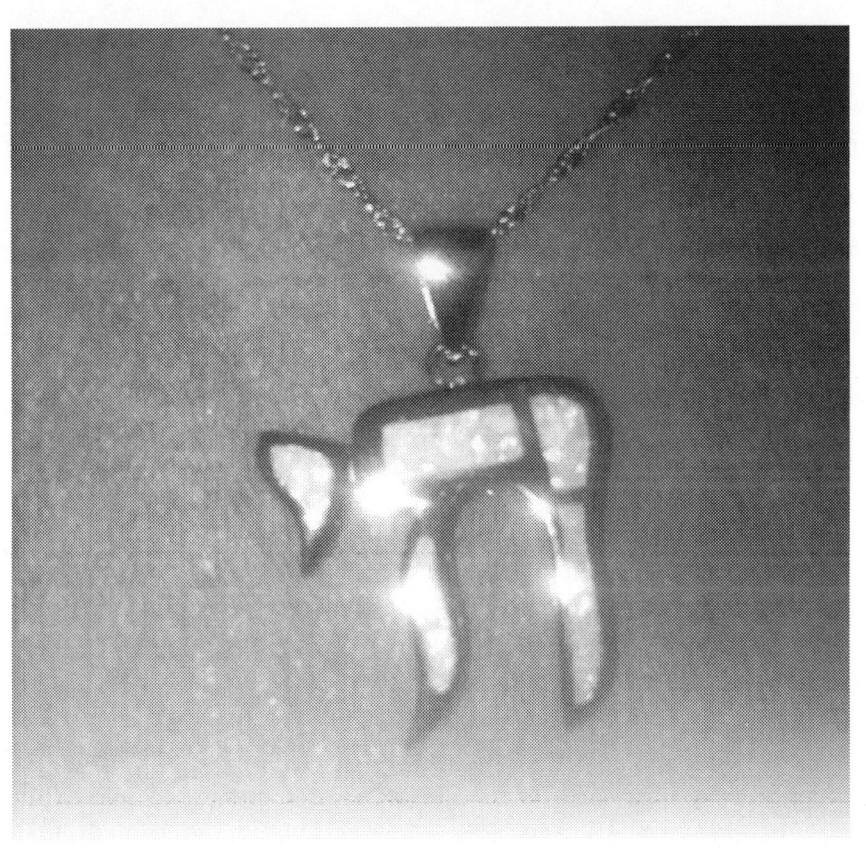

Chapter 5.5:

A Divine Message in Hebrew
Bev's New Hebrew word "Chai"
necklace, from our cruise ship.

In this chapter, I will explore an interval of time where I began experiencing revelations from God in ways I never dreamed possible. You may have noticed this is Chapter 5.5. It is not a typo! It is designated deliberately. Earlier on, I mentioned the significance of the number five as it occurred, and reoccurred, numerous times through-out our medical miracle. I would like to explain to you why this is so significant, at least to Bev and me and to many in the Jewish community who understand the significance of the Hebrew letter *"Hei."* In order to fully explain this, I must get a little technical and historical if you are to fully understand the background of the delivery of our revelation. This focus is necessary in order for me to fully share with you the events occurring between my fiftieth and fifty-fifth birthday.

Through the years, God has chosen many varied methods for communicating His divine will to humanity. These messages have varied greatly as God chose to speak to His servants at a time of need in the lives of His people. For Abraham, Lot, Moses, and Joshua their messages were delivered through the form of heavenly visitors. For Jacob and Joseph, their messages came in dreams or night visions. For many of the prophets, they were spoken to with an audible voice, at least audible to them. The prophets were instructed on specific messages they were to speak. But regardless of how God chose the do it, the most important fact is that they were divinely visited. The lives of these men had a very specific and divine purpose. God spoke to them directly and deliberately!

In the New Testament, the heavenly visitation was redefined somewhat as Jesus, the Word of God, came directly from heaven in the form of a man and tabernacled with the believers. This was similar yet very different from the time God tabernacled with the nation of Israel in His Shechinah glory in the wilderness. Through many signs and wonders, and acts of power, Jesus showed first hand evidence of what the power of God looks like. His temporal life reflected a power never witnessed by humanity. He then left with a promise that the Holy Spirit would come with power upon His followers and lead and guide them into all truth.

In essence, the indwelling Holy Spirit picked up where Jesus left off. Jesus had promised that His followers would do greater things than He. So, as the disciples traveled from place to place, they performed many miracles. These miracles were evidence that the Holy Ghost power of

God did indeed rest upon them. During their ministry, they not only performed many miracles but were also the beneficiaries of many miracle interventions. These miracles were necessary to enable them to complete their ordained tasks. The accounts of these miracles fill the pages of the New Testament and they leave the reader in amazement.

Historically, God has proven His desire to interact with His children. Is it too far out of line to suggest that God may still visit His children, in special and supernatural ways? Can He not use supernatural visitations to instruct us and prepare us for a specific task? Is this not how He glorifies Himself to the world? God has never surrendered to the will of humanity. He fully intends to complete His will upon the Earth. As the church age begins to wind down, and apostasy begins its grip on our world, is it inconceivable that God may once again visit those who are remaining faithful? Could He not do this through demonstrations of His divine power? His desire has always been to use human beings to influence the world in supernatural ways. Is He preparing us for what lies ahead, while giving warning to those who have refused to believe?

In much the same way the prophets had done, I believe God will continue to be a God of grace and continue to send those who will reach out with the truth. God would always tell the prophets before sending judgment, "I want them to know a prophet has been among them!" God will never judge a people who have not heard the truth and been given the opportunity to either accept or deny it.

I believe as we move closer and closer to the end, God will manifest Himself powerfully through His faithful people. I do emphasize "faithful!" He will complete His revelation of himself through those who are His chosen and who are a cleansed bride, without spot or blemish. We are His Holy Ghost resistance to an onslaught of evil like the world has never experienced. The times of the end, according to the book of Revelation, will see the world coming under the power of an antichrist, and he will fundamentally change the world. This leader will be much like the Nazi German leader, Adolf Hitler.....except on steroids! He will hate all Jewish people and Christians who trust and embrace the God of heaven. His sphere of influence will not be one nation, it will instead be one world..... Our world!

The truth of the matter is that God will convey His message to whomever He pleases and in whatever method He chooses. He will do this whether we believe He will or not. He does not, nor has He ever, sought our approval to act in the world. It is not our world. The Earth belongs to God. Everything in it is His and it always has been. If there is a need, He will meet it and in whatever way He chooses. This truth is not likely to change any time soon. For me, it took the events occurring two years ago for God to reveal His truth about my life to me personally. God revealed it in a way that changed my life's direction.

In this chapter, as I mentioned earlier, I want to take you through one specific interval of my life. I believe God used this interval to reveal Himself to me, and to my family. Others have been impacted and blessed in very special ways. Not one of us really understands the power of one act of faith. In reality, it may be the one act that God is waiting to see before He bestows blessings and purpose upon your life. There is no doubt that "faith" pleases Him. For me, there have been many things in my life that I am certain God did not and still does not like. I am an open book before Him. When I committed myself to God I gave Him my all…..good and bad. I trusted God to know exactly how to deal with my imperfections. I have found Him to be most faithful through all of my wavering.

God actually began preparing me for this revelation two years before I turned fifty. It occurred as a result of coming to some pretty ugly spiritual conclusions about my own life. After many years of servitude to God and His church, I realized there was much more that He wanted me to see. There was much more He wanted me to say and to teach. God was calling me out and wanted a response as to whether I would be faithful to His calling. Unfortunately, I was reluctant to answer right away. This was a regretful mistake, in light of the promise I had made Him many years earlier…..“That I would follow wherever He led.” It was not long before I started feeling His response.

His first call on my life came in the form of physical illness. I was diagnosed with deep vein thrombosis in 2010. It sidelined me for a period of time and gave me plenty of time to contemplate my life and relationship to Him. His main message was for me to put aside any pre-conceived religious notions and to—seek Him out in the old paths. In other words, He was calling me to go back and revisit the things that had come before.

This opened up my pathway to a whole new commitment to study and learn everything that I could about His divine workings. God convicted me for not allowing Him to guide my study and prayer life as He desired. I was spending way too much time in the commentaries. I needed to be spending time on my knees and trusting the Spirit to teach me. He reminded me that Jesus was Jewish. If I really wanted to understand the full impact of what Jesus was teaching, and the interpretations of His Words, I must understand it in light of His Jewishness.

In the spirit of pursuing God, I began to study every book I could get my hands on concerning Judaism and the prevailing religion at the time of Christ. I began to study Hebrew at a local conservative synagogue. The Cantor would meet with us every Tuesday night. He would spend an hour teaching us the significance of messages of the prayer book and the services surrounding the holy days of the Jews. We attended a Jewish Pesach (Passover) meal with the congregation. This was one of the most powerfully "spiritual" experiences I have ever had. The time we spent with Him as well as the opportunities we had to sit down with the Rabbis, opened up our hearts and minds like nothing else. In the end, God did something in my heart and mind that opened up my life for a whole new level of interaction. This is something I did not realize at the time. These months of study were the most spiritually enriching of my life.

The study of Hebrew is fascinating. The Hebrew language and alphabet, by themselves, are fascinating things. As I studied in those days, I learned much about the contemporary Jewish religion of the day. It is divided into three distinct movements, the Reform (Liberal), Conservative (Mainstream), and Orthodox (Ultra Conservative). I had also gotten involved, a few years before, with a group of Noahides. They were a very small group in our local area and were primarily focused on the seven laws that God gave Noah. It was with this group that I was most challenged to remove my religious blinders. It was a delightfully "uncomfortable" experience for me. In this study, I first learned about a mystical, or spiritual, form of Jewishness. This new teaching, I discovered, probably influences much of the thought processes throughout the various forms of the Jewish religion. It is called Kabbalah.

Kabbalah can be thought of as the mystical or spiritual tool for interpretation of the truths of Judaism and the Jewish scripture. For me, it was the common denominator between the two schools of thought, Jewish and Christian. Unlike the main tenants of Judaism, Kabbalah is about personal relationship with God and all of His creation. It is not a system of laws that dictates your behavior. The purpose of Kabbalah is to open the door to finding answers, as to the divine purpose of our lives, on a personal level. This is something every born again believer should thirst for. Kabbalah was a very guarded tool in the very earliest of times. It was forbidden for a man to study Kabbalah until after his fortieth birthday.

I found the spiritual tenants and goals of Kabbalah more relative to the doctrine of Christ than any other aspect of Judaism. I believe it provides a structure complimenting Christianity, taking faith by the hand. As I began this deeper journey into the religion of Jesus, it resulted in tangible and applicable revelations. The whole of my life started changing! I began to have a clearer understanding. When I was first exposed to Kabbalah, I thought these strange teachers were kooks.

To the Cabbalist, the Word of God is a very real and tangible reality. In the beginning, God spoke and as His Words came out they went forth with all the force of His divine will. In power, they accomplished His purpose.....creating the Earth and all that fill it. Again, God said "Let there be" and "there was". The Words to Cabbalist are made up of the Hebrew alphabet and was divinely taught to the first man by the angels. In essence, the Hebrew alphabet is the language of the angels.....from the divine realm. This language includes a numeric value given to each letter of the Hebrew alphabet. It is this concept that has been popularized, more recently by the medium of books and movies, depicting revelation through the "Bible Code." These letters are not only characters in the alphabet as our A-B-C's. Instead, they are a symbolic design. They represent certain aspects of the divine character of God Himself. They are pictorials of God's character and of man's interactions with Him. During this period of study, Bev came across a book of the Hebrew letters and their numeric values. She presented it to me as a gift.

I have been most amazed by the numeric assignment to each letter of the Hebrew Alphabet. I applied it to the recent events of healing and the past years of my life. As you might have guessed, I have evaluated one specific letter from the Hebrew alphabet. My evaluation has been of the Hebrew letter *"Hei"*, and it represents the number five. I believe you will agree with me, after you see the numerous recurrences of this divine number, that my observations are far too many to be considered mere coincidence. For me, it is affirmation that God is in full control and is ever present in the lives of His faithful. The remainder of this chapter will focus on the spiritual meaning of the letter *"Hei"* representing the number five. I will walk you through the times it has appeared in real life circumstances over the five years between my fiftieth and fifty-fifth birthday. Let me begin!

In the year of 2008, I celebrated my fiftieth (5x10) birthday. In her usual fashion, my sweet wife wanted to make this a very special occasion for me and the family. She reserved a special place for us to spend the weekend with our children. This special place was the Bluff View Inn, located in the Bluff View Art District, in Chattanooga. We had my 50th birthday celebration with all the kids and grandkids. It was a very special time. That night, Bev's gift to me was a ring that she had designed and was custom made at a local jeweler. The ring is a gold Magen David (Star of David, literally Shield of David) and overlaid with the cross of Christ. It represented the revelations we had been receiving over the past several years. It was a reminder of the inseparable nature and purpose of the nation of Israel and the Church of Jesus Christ. It is a tangible reminder of God's overarching plan for salvation. The ring is a constant reminder of this truth.

On Saturday morning, we all gathered at one of the fine restaurants in the district and enjoyed a fantastic breakfast. Even though I had a mild cold, the weekend was perfect! At the time, I was not acquainted with any of the family that owned the art district. Many months later, I came to realize that it was a member of that family that had become the vessel God used to bring about my healing. At the time of my fiftieth birthday, I was not aware that I needed a healing. It would be almost five years later that I would walk into the office of the man, Dr. Portera, who became my surgeon. There was a building across from the Bed and Breakfast where we stayed. Dr. Portera would later share memories of that building with us from his years as a school boy. On that special fiftieth birthday, God connected us and we were totally unaware.

In the year 2010 (5x402), we experienced the second event in our journey to revelation. It came in the form of a deep vein thrombosis (blood clot in my leg) as I have mentioned before. This event was significant to me because I had never had a serious ailment that was even remotely life threatening. Now, for a period of time, I would be laid up and on a series of Lovenox injections. Lovenox is a low molecular weight heparin that my nurse/wife would administer daily into my stomach. It was during this period of time that I became seriously aware of my own mortality. It was here that my true pursuit of God and His truth took on new fervor. As I look back, I am also amazed! In my fifty-fifth year of life, I would encounter a massive saddle clot after surgery. I would learn that I am allergic to heparin, a condition called (HIT). At this point in time, in 2010, my allergy to Heparin did not to exist.

Then came the year 2013, the fifth (5) year leading up to my fifty-fifth (5x11) birthday. If I had any idea what God had planned for this special year, I would have panicked big time. Not knowing the future is a wonderful thing. In 2013, God showered my life with revelation. On June 5th (5), Bev and I returned from our Florida vacation. I came back with a new sensation that I was feeling in my side. It was forty-five (5x9) days later that I was diagnosed with a mass on my pancreas. Ten (5x2) days after my diagnosis, I was in the office of the man who would do my surgery for pancreatic cancer, the Whipple Procedure. A Whipple Procedure, otherwise known as a pancreaticoduodenectomy, involves removing the head of the pancreas, the gall bladder, part of the duodenum which is a part of the small intestine, a small portion of the stomach, and lymph nodes near the head of the pancreas. Then, everything is reconnected to form a new system.

Before scheduling the surgery, I ask for a few days to get physically prepared. I worked out and took five (5) days off from work so I would be rested. We were working ten hours per day at the time. It was exactly forty (5x8) days from diagnosis to surgery. Then came the surgery, lasting five and a half hours (5.5). After a night in the MICU, I was taken the next day to the surgical floor where I would recover until discharged. I recovered on the 5th floor for the next ten days (5x2). On Sept 6, I got up early. I was waiting for a visit from Dr. Portera's nurse, Deanna, to release me to go home. Deanna was delayed due to an unexpected meeting. During this time of waiting, I went into respiratory distress. My lungs were totally blocked, a saddle clot. And, the adventure had begun!

The next thing I remember was waking up five (5) days later. A machine had been doing my breathing for me for those five days. It was weird. Those five (5) days can only be described by others.....family, friends, and those who provided treatment. Here is what I have been told. After the saddle clot formed in my lungs, the blood could no longer push through. My heart became tired and after the use of a clot buster..... my heart stopped beating. I underwent intensive CPR in the MICU by a team of medical professionals for fifty-five (5x11) minutes. According to my surgeon, I was administered several trays and three crash carts of medicines. A clot busting treatment was brought from the pharmacy and given to me in the MICU. I understand that this procedure was rarely, if ever done, in the MICU setting. I was too unstable to be taken to radiology which was the normal routine. On this particular day, there were five (5) doctors in a meeting in MICU. All five doctors responded to the code. I was later told by one of the attending nurses that he could count on one hand the number of times in the last ten years that all five doctors had been at the hospital at the same time.

Twenty days later (5x4), I was released from the hospital to go home. I was released directly from the MICU. Being released directly from MICU, without first going to a floor for observation, is highly unusual. From there, my period of recovery began. Fifty-five (5x11) days later, on November 19, I returned to work on a part-time basis. Five (5) days after that, I reached my fifty-fifth (5x11) birthday. My five year odyssey had finally come to fruition and I was left a completely different man. Twenty-five (5x5) days after that, I went back to work full time.

Thanks for bearing with me through the recap but now comes the good part! A few weeks later, we went for our first return doctors visit with my surgeon, Dr. Portera. While we were out that day, I got a call from a reporter from our local NBC affiliate, Matt Barbour. Matt had heard of our story and he wanted to do an interview. We agreed to meet that day at a local coffee house that agreed to let us set up the camera for the interview. During the interview, there was one specific question he emphasized that left me pondering. The question was, "Why fifty-five minutes?" It was a very good question because, in my understanding, fifty-five minutes is not the typical "code blue" protocol. I have been told that a person in the condition that I was in would most likely have brain injury after fifteen minutes. The end result would be permanent brain damage if not death.

When I got home that day, and after a period of pondering the question, I remembered the Hebrew alphabet. Bev and I read about the Hebrew letter *"Hei"*, the number five, from the book she had given me as a gift. At the time I had not put together any of the information that I have shared with you. It was my first attempt in seeking for what God was indeed trying to say. What I discovered blew me away! As I have gone back and reviewed what has transpired through it all, I continue to be in awe.

The first thing I learned was the letter *"Hei"* connotes divine revelation. The sound of the letter, when used in conversation, is one of a mere exhalation. It teaches that focusing on the breath is a means of spiritual development. In the larger picture, *"Hei"* reflects the effortless breath of God when creating Adam. *"Hei"* represents a means of attaining a lofty perspective. It alludes to the five (5) dimensions of the human soul; nefesh (physical instincts), ruach (emotions), neshamah (the mind), chayah (bridge to transcendental awareness), and yechidah (spiritual unity). These are the things that define the whole life of a man.

When Moses was receiving his charge to go get God's children out of Egypt, Moses ask God, "Who shall I tell them has sent me?" God's answer, tell them "I am" sent you. In Hebrew, this name is considered the most sacred name of God. It is the tetragrammaton and is more commonly known today as Yahweh (Yud, *"Hei"*, Vov, *"Hei"*). In essence, the letter *"Hei"*, the number five (5), appears twice in this sacred name of God as well as the other sacred name Jehovah. This makes me want to shout out another Hebrew word where *"Hei"* appears twice, Hallelujah!.....this is the highest expression of praise, joy, and thanksgiving to an awesome God.

During this time, I had learned Dr. Portera experienced his fiftieth (5x10) birthday. I have rejoiced as I have seen how this ordeal has changed his life. He has blessed our heart so much. Bev and I celebrated our twentieth (5x4) wedding anniversary on October 10, 2013. We had planned a European cruise for our twentieth anniversary. Due to my recovery from surgery, our cruise had to be canceled. We spent our twentieth (5x4) anniversary close to home.....at the Back Inn Café, in the Bluff View Art District. At the time, we were still unaware of Dr. Portera's connection to the Art District.

In 2014, we took a European cruise for our twenty-first wedding anniversary. We had an awesome experience on the ship. On the very first day of the cruise, while browsing in one of the shops, we came upon a pendent. The pendant was the Hebrew word *"Chai"*. We looked throughout the entire shop and even asked the attendant if they had any more Hebrew letters or words. They did not! Needless to say, Bev wears this necklace today! This Hebrew word is understood to represent "Life or Living." The Hebrew word *shehecheyanu* in the single word form means, *"who has kept us alive."* Following that word to its root, verb form, is *Cheit-yod-"hei"* meaning "to live." This further breaks down to the root word, *chai,* meaning "life or living." As we celebrated our twenty-first anniversary, the necklace seemed to be God's confirmation of His true gift to us.....Life!

God has convinced us that He is actively working in our lives, and we have been excited to share our experiences with you. He used something tangible, yet spiritually connected to His holy people of Israel, to speak to our hearts and to the hearts of others. He is God! He can do that. One of the key messages of the letter *"Hei"* is the message of divine revelation through the breath of God. The message in the letter *"Hei"* has helped me to understand how I could cease breathing for almost an hour but experience no ill effects. I had perfectly normal brain activity upon evaluation. When I had no breath of my own, He loaned me His! God is so amazing, and His ways are passed finding out. His purposes are secure, and His will cannot be hindered. Praise His name on high!!

Chapter Six

Touching God, a Quest for Intimacy

"In all of our religious efforts, is getting closer to God our primary focus or are we serving Him from a distance with no expectation of ever achieving real intimacy?

Moses sat on the mountainside speaking to God. God was preparing to visit the entire nation of Israel. Moses was captivated by this special holy moment. He asked God a very revealing question. He had come so near to God, and he wanted to see His face. Moses wanted to speak to God as he would to a man. God's answer to him was very revealing.

> (Ex 33:20-23 NKJV) 20 But He said, "You cannot see My face; for no man shall see Me, and live." 21 And the LORD said, "Here is a place by Me, and you shall stand on the rock. 22 So it shall be, while My glory passes by, that I will put you in the cleft of the rock, and will cover you with My hand while I pass by. 23 Then I will take away My hand, and you shall see My back; but My face shall not be seen."

Many years later, the apostle James wrote an inspired truth specifically to those who may wish to get close to God, much the same way as Moses. His message was a simple one. It is a message I have alluded to already, but it bears repeating. "Draw near to God and He will draw near to you….. (James 4:8 NKJV). I believe this passage. In fact, I take it literally. God knows our hearts and if intimacy with Him is your heart's desire, there is nothing on earth that will keep it from happening. In the interaction between God and Moses, it appears to me that God was more than willing to show himself to Moses when He knew it was the desire of his heart. There were things Moses did not understand. As long as we are robed in the human flesh, there always will be. God was telling him that the day Moses would be able to look upon His face would be the day he would lay down this fleshly robe and walk into eternity. This thought is both glorious and chilling!

Now, let us bring this discussion down to our modern age. How badly do we desire to see and know God? In all of our religious efforts, is getting closer to God our primary focus or are we serving Him from a distance with no expectation of ever achieving intimacy? Sadly, for many believers I am afraid this is exactly the case. We see God as being way up there while we are locked in our own little world way down here. We see ourselves as poor and sinful creatures. We see ourselves unworthy of a touch of divinity.

Therefore, we neglect to pursue a relationship. We spend our time doing good "religious stuff" in hopes of somehow gaining God's favor.

The truth is, we are locked in our own little world. We are locked here with the presence of His Holy Spirit all around us and within us if we have received Him. We are poor sinful creatures who are unworthy of a taste of sweet divinity. This has never deterred the Father from caring for us, imparting spiritual gifts, and sending the provisions we need for salvation in spiritual power. I might add, this all came at a great cost to Him! Oh how much He must love His children—His creation!

For those who have a true desire to get intimate with the Father, there is a pathway that will lead you closer. However, we will never get close enough in this life. I am not there myself, and I will never be close enough as long as I am in this life. It is because I have seen and witnessed His presence in ways previously unimaginable to me! As it is with most of our concepts about God and His person, intimacy with Him is not as difficult as we make it. We must get passed the doctrine from the devils of hell which imply that we must do good works in order to gain the favor of God. In moving beyond this fallacy, we will be well on our way to a true relationship with Him.

Our works (righteousness) are as filthy rags to Him (Isa. 64:6 NKJV), regardless of how good we think they might be. As I have heard it said many times, "We do not do good works in order to get to heaven, we do good works because we are going to heaven!"

There are three gifts compelling us toward a true relationship with God. It requires only one act on our part to experience them. What is that act? We must deliberately and humbly receive the gifts! The most powerful act we can perform to gain access to God and have perfect communion and fellowship with Him is to receive the gifts He has made available to us. I know this flies in the face of all the religious "do's" and "don'ts" that have been drilled into our minds from a very early age.

Receiving God's gifts however, must also come with a disclaimer. It is not as cut and dry as it may appear. You cannot receive anything from God unless you believe He is indeed God. Therefore, faith is the required element for receiving these gifts and pleasing God. The scripture states, "But without faith, it is impossible to please Him….. (Heb. 11:6 NKJV)"

In the modern world, we use the term "faith" loosely because of the programmed religious mindset we have. It should be emphasized that our faith must be placed in God and the finished work of Jesus alone. God did not tell us we must have faith in our religious leaders or our particular denomination in order to please Him. To misplace our faith into those things is as much idolatry as the worship of Baal or Moloch, the sun god!

What are the three mysterious gifts that will guarantee an intimate relationship to the Creator of Heaven and Earth? In essence, they are not mysterious at all. They are spiritual but not mysterious. God has taken great pains to make sure we could understand them. I suppose the best place to begin is in the beginning! I love the way the gospel of John begins. John was inspired to make the gifts of God so clear that even a child could understand them. It is in his message that the works of the Father, things done on our behalf, are made crystal clear to us.

John 1: 1-2, 14, 32 (NKJV)

Gift One: (John 1: 1 NKJV) In the beginning was the Word, and the Word was with God, and the Word was God. 2 He was in the beginning with God.

(Gen 1:1 NKJV) In the beginning God created the heavens and the earth. 2 The earth was without form, and void; and darkness was on the face of the deep. And the Spirit of God was hovering over the face of the waters. 3 Then God said, "Let there be light"; and there was light.

And God said, "let there be..............!"

There you have it! The earth was without form, void, and dark before the first Word was uttered. It was not until God said, "Let there be".…... that there was! Of all entities existing anywhere in heaven or earth, the Words of God reign supreme in power. For when God utters His mind and His will, it is immediately accomplished. The spirits and angels stand at attention when He beckons. They respond immediately as He commands. His Word is not a suggestion or a request. It becomes an instant reality when He speaks. It has always been so and it will always be. This is something we should never doubt or forget.

In fact, there is a little known sect or mystical doctrine that is prevalent in Judaism. This is the mystical doctrine known as Kabbalah that I have mentioned in the previous chapter. In Kabbalah, the Words of God are like super powered agents of change and ministry. If you can picture it, it is as though when He speaks these agents go forth from His mouth to accomplish His dictates. Unlike us, if we want something done we either do it ourselves or we convince others to do it for us. With God, no convincing is required. He speaks the Word and it is done. With this in mind, we can get a whole new vision of the significance of what Jesus said when being tempted by Satan during the wilderness fast. "It is written, man shall not live by bread alone, but by every Word that proceeds from the mouth of God!" (Mat.4:4 NKJV)

When I think of the way God has intervened throughout human history, it mystifies me to think He went to the trouble of leaving a written record of it all. He left a record of the part He wants us to know. It must be emphasized, God wants us to know and experience the power of His Words! He wants us to know the joy He felt at the Creation. He wants us to know His disappointment when man fell into sin. He wants us to know His anger at demonic perversions that have caused Him to send the great floods of water and fire. This is an anger that will soon cause Him to judge all of the nations, in these end times, with all manner of tribulations. He also wants us to know His willingness to give grace and forgiveness. He wants us to know His grace. He wants us to know His mercies that we witnessed so clearly in the person of Jesus Christ. He has intervened so that we might experience life more abundantly.

An old backwoods preacher was preaching a revival meeting that I was attending. During his sermon, he paused and let silence fall over the congregation. He then held up his big "ole" Bible and made a very clear proclamation. He said, "Do you see this Bible? (Everyone nodded to affirm.) This is not everything God knows (he had my attention), but it is everything God wants you to know!" Of all the messages I have ever heard, this statement started me on a life-long quest to know what God wants ME to know. His statement was, and has continued to be, a powerful motivational force for me.

There is no way we can read through the Old Testament without gaining a clear picture of God's person, His divine will, and His innermost desires. Specifically, we find a picture of those things that are in His heart for the care of mankind. It all culminates in the life and doctrine of Christ. It is in perfect agreement with the Old Testament as revealed in the New Testament. In the life of Jesus, God shows us the great price He is willing to pay to have restoration with His human creation. When John introduced the Word (Jesus) in verse one, it should be noted that he ascribed it a gender, "He was in the beginning with God. All things were made through Him!….." (John 1:2-3 NKJV)

It seems as wonderful as the gift of the written Word is, in accomplishing these special things in our lives, it is not enough. In every generation throughout the centuries, Satan has taken this gift and bent it to His own petty and perverted desires. He has left it distorted and made it to serve his own appetites. This is Satan's best and most effective attempt at robbing God of all the glory He deserves from humanity. He did it through the hearts and words of those who have become his mouthpieces, his puppets. Unfortunately, this distortion has resulted in many religious perversions. These perversions have tarnished the character of God before people as well as the children of God. It has caused many of His to reject Him or fall short of the life He has chosen for them. As a result, a second gift was required to defend and maintain the divine purity of the original message!

> Gift Two: John 1:14 NKJV And the Word became flesh
> and dwelt among us, and we beheld His glory, the glory
> of the only begotten of the Father, full of grace and truth.

In the life and message of Jesus, the mystery of God's revelation continues in the form of a sinless man. This man is inspired and motivated by only one thing, the Word, the message of His Father. The world of the Israelites was in desperate need of a religious correction. Remember, Israel is God's chosen people. They are to be used by Him to reveal Himself to the entire world. Their system of religion had become one that had burdened the people rather than free them. Their system of embellished laws had choked the people, spiritually speaking, and had created a system failing to meet the intent of its designer, God. God was not being honored, and the message was being perverted. God's people were not living in the fullness of relationship that divinity desired. So to correct the situation, as John reported, "The Word became flesh and dwelt among us!"

With the gift of Jesus, God sent the great correction that Israel and the gentile world needed. Finally, there was a living and breathing being. He would not distort the truth for His own personal gain. He was there in the beginning with God and was birthed spiritually in heaven when the Father's Words were first uttered. Interpretation of scripture was not a problem for Him. He was the scripture. Unfortunately, His interpretation was a problem for the imposters in the temple. It revealed their spiritual arrogance and ignorance. It resulted in the many deceptions of the people. This supernatural enlightenment can be seen in Jesus as a small boy. As a small boy, He stood in the synagogue teaching the leaders. They were amazed at His doctrine and His authority to speak and address the spiritual deficiencies of His day.

Jesus set the religious world on its heels. He did not obey their well-intentioned but embellished laws. He chose to obey the laws of God in their original intent and from the context they were originally given. The religious leaders of His day had to admit, ".....no man ever spoke like this man" (John 7:46 NKJV). A few of the religious leaders secretly believed His message. However, they were compelled to keep their secret faith hidden from those who were propagating a different truth. (Keeping in mind, any different truth is by definition a lie!) To unbelievers or commoners, and foreigners, Jesus was divinely different from anyone they had ever met or heard.

Looking back through history, Jesus emerges as the one man who has yielded the greatest impact on humanity. He never traveled the world. Instead, He chose to inspire those in His closest circles, those in His own back yard. In turn, all those He inspired went into the world spreading His special and powerful message. Today, His name is known throughout the world. Not only is it known, but the forces of evil are still actively engaged in a battle to stomp out the doctrine of this obscure carpenter from Nazareth. Those enemies still have not succeeded in their tasks, nor will they ever. It is sad to see the puny efforts we make in the church to actually resist the enemy. We should be making a spectacle of ourselves, if necessary, in order to make a difference in the lives of people.

Jesus turned the world on its heels by living a life of grace and truth as "The Word made Flesh." He allowed himself to be crucified by those whom He had rebuked and warned, the religious imposters. Through political maneuvering, they compelled the forces of Rome to do their dirty work. He faced the cruelty of these evil men with all of the pain they could inflict. He understood this to be the natural reaction of evil to truth. He knew death could not and would not hold Him. He was there in the beginning, and He knew He would be there in the end. Truthfully, knowing this should help us to be better prepared for persecutions. The more scripturally sound our lives are the more Satan is riled.

After three days, Jesus walked out of His grave. He showed Himself to His disciples and began to prepare them for what lay ahead. He understood that they would be taking up the mantle He had given them. They would be the ones charged with taking His abundant "grace and truth" to the world. He knew they would meet the same resistance that He had, and it would eventually lead them all to severe persecution or a martyr's death.

I believe they fully understood this and were willing to make the sacrifice. It is still true in today's world. Those who choose to live by the unadulterated truth of God's Word will run the same risk. It is a scriptural promise that we will be persecuted, mocked, ridiculed, and even sometimes killed for the sake of truth.

In order to enable His followers to have the power and spiritual fortitude to accomplish His task, He supplied to them one more gift. Fifty days after Jesus walked out of His grave, they received that gift. The last gift was the Father to complete the plan of salvation. The gift remains one of the most misunderstood abused aspects of the salvation experience for mankind! From the time this gift was given, God made His dwelling place in the hearts of those who are willing to fully receive Him and His Holiness.

> Gift Three: John 1:32 NKJV And John bore witness saying "I saw the Spirit descending from heaven like a dove, and he remained on Him.

The scene at Jesus' baptism is really important for modern day believers. It marks the only time, it can be said, that a man actually saw the presence of the Holy Spirit.....at least in the New Testament era. There it is, the Holy Spirit descended out of heaven and rested upon Jesus as He was raised from His baptismal waters. For all believers, this scene marks the time when the gifts of God were unified in purpose to bring about salvation for all humanity. Jesus was indeed armed, empowered, and inspired by the presence of His Holy Spirit and remained so throughout His earthly ministry. In this scene, we witness the Word and the Spirit becoming one in the Son.

The fact that the spirit remained on Him, is of great significance. This marked a change of direction. It began a new era. Instead of the spirit coming upon a man intermittently to accomplish God's will, the Holy Spirit would now dwell within him. He would be a constant source of power and guidance. God knows, that alone, we do not stand a chance against the forces of Satan. We must have the ever present, enlightening, and sustaining power of the Holy Spirit. The disciples would realize this. The risen Lord had instructed them to, ".....tarry ye in the city of Jerusalem, until you be endued with power from on high."(Luke 24:49 KJV) On the day of Pentecost (Fifty days after Passover and the Resurrection), as they sat in the upper room, they learned specifically what Jesus meant. The third gift came in power and holiness. The lives of the disciples and all those they touched were never the same again.

Another significant fact, about this spirit of revelation at the baptism of Christ, is that the spirit began His work immediately. His first order of business was to serve notice to Satan, the prince of the power of the air. Jesus was led into the wilderness to face the father of all desolations and there He met Satan. Despite all of Satan's cunning and deception, Jesus defeated him. His weapon you may ask?.....the Word of God.

After Pentecost, the changed lives of the disciples "in the Spirit" drew the attention of the religious leaders, as did their Lord. The change in them set up a new and immediate satanic persecution resulting in much bloodshed and the scattering of the disciples. Nothing in history has ever upset Satan's agenda like the day of Pentecost. Suddenly, mere men who were previously weak and submissive were now bold, empowered, and invisible to him through the Spirit. Satan now found himself an outcast in what he considered his own world. After the coming of the Spirit, when

Satan would try to barge into a man's life, He would find God there. God would promptly "kick him to the curb!"

Satan is powerless to resist. He and all his demons are subject to the Word that indwells the believer. They cannot change it! When Jesus walked out of the wilderness, back to complete His mission to humanity, Satan's days were numbered and he knew it. When the Holy Spirit came down on the day of Pentecost, Satan knew he no longer held the monopoly for humanities souls. He had no influence and no power over this Spirit filled, Spirit led man. It is the same for everyone that will accept the finished work of Christ. It is true for those that are willing to receive the Holy Spirit as their sole guide, and power source, for living in this modern world. Believe it! Satan's only weapon is to deceive us into believing there is another way to God. His effort is to get us to take our eyes off of the finished work of Calvary and Pentecost.

The spiritual scene of the baptism of the Spirit was on full display the day of Pentecost. The city was full of foreigners who became witness to the awesome power and effect of the coming of the Spirit. Although they came to town bringing many foreign gods and superstitions, many of them left town having received a touch from heaven. They became the first missionaries. The third gift was now given and the awesome power of God had now been entrusted to dwell within people. Knowing this truth leaves every true believer of Christ with no excuse for failure. We will have no acceptable excuses for having failed in our divine mission on the day when we see God face to face!

These are the very important things we must take away from the provisions God has abundantly given. He has made His heart, mind, and will for mankind abundantly clear to us. The first clarification was in the act of creation and then as He dealt with sinful humanity throughout the Old Testament. He sent to us the Word made flesh as a second clarification. His Son embodied every Word that was ever spoken by Him, in all of its power and purity. Finally, He sent the enabler.....His Holy Spirit. He was the divine teacher that would lead and guide all believers into spiritual truth and power.

An unworthy and powerless people may now live a supernatural existence, demonstrating the power of God to the world on a daily basis. "God forgive us if we fail, for we have no legitimate excuses. If we truly want intimacy with you there is nothing powerful enough to keep us from having it!"

There are not enough words in the English vocabulary to describe what Christ has accomplished on our behalf. It is my belief that most "believers" who have really been touched by Christ and His Holy Spirit are much like the blind man Jesus healed. The blind man did not know much about this man called Jesus. He could only report what he had experienced. He answered and said, "Whether He is a sinner or not I do not know. One thing I know: that though I was blind, now I see." (John 9:25 NKJV) The blind man did not know how it was or how it could have been, but he knew for sure that it was real. This is a great picture of what faith looks like.

When it comes to the gifts we have received, my position is the same as that of the blind man. We can never explain it, but we know deep in our heart it is real. The spoken Word of God became a living and breathing reality. Jesus lived the Word fully. He proclaimed it perfectly in the face of all manner of religious perversions and evils. The Holy Spirit then empowered all who would hear and believe Him. God sent them throughout the world to proclaim this truth. This is all we will ever need to know.

The Holy Spirit within the believer is the culmination of the work and plan of Almighty God. God effectively dealt with the sin of our first parents in the garden. We now have the power within us to resist the deceptions of the serpent. We have the power to interpret the actions and motives in others and to discern the difference between good and evil. We have the power to discern evil that is cloaked in a veil of good, for example, "the wolf in sheep's clothing." The Spirit indwells us as a sustaining presence. We will never need to fear a day when God is not present in our lives. The most powerful impact of such a gift is that it enables us to love others unconditionally, even though many times they make it hard for us to do so. God knows this love is the most powerful force in our arsenal. When everything else falls short it will turn wayward hearts to Him.

Now, I would challenge you to evaluate your relationship with God. How much do you really love God? Intimacy is not a one way street. God will always love you but intimacy cannot happen until you love Him back! This means that instead of going about your own business and doing whatever comes to mind, you instead, go about seeking to do

His business and whatever is on His mind. It means when you run up against the hardships and confusions of life that you refuse to lean on your own understanding and wisdom. Instead, you learn to lean on His Word and Spirit to guide your steps. Probably, the hardest of all is to love your fellow man by substituting God's truth "in grace" in place of your own judgments. Attempting to live the Christian life, a God centered life, is the most unnatural thing any human being can attempt. There will be many failures, but God will honor our motives and visit His power upon us whenever we stand in need. I am absolutely certain of this!

Chapter Seven

Man's Search for Significance

"Those who lust for power are never
satisfied, it seems to establish and exercise
control over other human beings is the
ultimate power "fix" for them. TLD

**Photo of: Beautiful Blarney Castle, County
Cork, Ireland. Used by permission.**

Ants or People, a Matter of Perspective

I have lived here in the south for my entire life. I have enjoyed a rather laid back and hassle free existence. For the past twenty years or so, give or take a few years, I have been learning to deal with a new and pesky little critter, Fire Ants. I am not quite sure where they came from, other than further down south. I do not know exactly how they got here. I do know where I wish they would go! However, it is clear they keep expanding their boundaries. I have now found myself locked in mortal combat to maintain complete and full control of my lawn. These are some resilient little creatures and quite painful if one does not watch their step when they venture outdoors.

Anyway, my wife and I have employed several methods in an effort to eradicate these little devils from the lawn. Nothing we have done has been profoundly successful. I tried using the various poisons that were available, but I swear, I can hear them chuckling as they drag these tasty morsels back into their hill for dinner. I have tried burning them out. Yes, that is right. I pour gasoline into their hill and stand back, tossing a flame in the general direction and poof, there it goes. This action does a pretty good job of eradication but leaves a big brown spot where grass now refuses to grow. I think I am defeating my purpose.

Finally I arrived at a compromising solution. I will not try to kill them. Instead, I will really annoy them. I will make it unpleasant for them to live in my yard. I do not want to destroy them. I only want them to build anywhere but my yard. My first plan of attack consists of driving the lawnmower onto the top of the hill and smashing it into the ground. As those little red pests start screaming out in protest, pouring out of their hill, I back up and pull over the spot with the blades running wide open. I sit there while they experience a bit of turbulence. This always seems to do it. They pack their little ant bags and set out on a journey, to a faraway country, where no lawn mowers can wreck their day. Victory is mine, at least until I see the signs of their new mound in progress on the other side of the lawn. A faraway country to them is still my front yard. Oh well, start up the lawn mower, let us keep them moving. At least if I stay vigilant, I will have a lawn where grass will grow and is devoid of those big brown spots where I rained down fire and brimstone on their heads.

Then one day it hits me. How many times do we as human beings drive our stakes into a place where God does not want us to be? Just as the ants, we do not even consider who owns the property on which we choose to build our house or our life. We just build. In essence, we all live in God's yard. Regardless of where we choose to build, it is all His. He has a justifiable say in exactly where we are to end up. If it takes pulling His Holy Ghost lawnmower over our hill, He will not hesitate to do it. We may come out with fist in the air and curse the day, but it makes no difference. If He wants us to move, we will move!

The Bible is choked full of evidence of what I say is true. At Babel, God visited and created chaos in order to move humanity and bring about the creation of the nations. In the call of Abraham, God moves him to a place he had never been in order to bring about the creation of His chosen people. In Moses, God moved His people in order to deliver them from their slavery and to create a spiritual household that would be peculiar to all other peoples. In Joshua, God moved His people in order for the world to see His power to deliver and to save. In Jesus, God moved His Son from heaven to earth in order to set the record straight, to highlight the truth of salvation to the whole world. Even though God owns it all, He has stayed quite busy keeping things moving to His desired end…..and quite effectively I might add!

As humans, we should work much harder to try to see ourselves as God sees us. We have no authority to dictate our terms to Him, any more than the ants dictate their terms to us. As surely as God brought salvation to the whole world, He allowed persecution to scatter the church to the uttermost parts of the earth, so that the whole world could know Him. It is His lawn, He can do as he pleases. There is coming a time for the fire and brimstone but not now. For now, we live. Hopefully we are living in the place He has chosen for us. Even so, we may still experience the pain of an evil world that despises our presence. But believe me, this is nothing when compared to facing an angry God who despises our rebellion.

Genesis 11: 1—7 (NKJV) 1 Now the whole earth had one language and one speech. 2 And it came to pass, as they journeyed from the east, that they found a plain in the land of Shinar, and they dwelt there. 3 Then they said to one another, "Come, let us make bricks and bake them thoroughly." They had brick for stone, and they had asphalt for mortar. 4 And they said, "Come, let us build ourselves a city, and a tower whose top is in the heavens; let us make a name for ourselves, lest we be scattered abroad over the face of the whole earth." 5 But the LORD came down to see the city and the tower that the sons of men had built. 6 And the LORD said, "Indeed the people are one and they all have one language, and this is what they begin to do; now nothing that they propose to do will be withheld from them. 7 Come, let Us go down and there confuse their language, that they may not understand one another's speech."

Up until now, I have dedicated most of my time talking about the fact that God visits us, as individuals, in order to establish and affirm our relationship with Himself. Personally, there have been many divine appointments in my life, as I am sure there are with many of those who may read this book. There is another, larger perspective concerning divine appointments that is very, very, important to the world, especially today! From the very beginning of time, God has visited the world performing divine acts on behalf of humanity. He will continue to do so until the very end.

Those visits were not and are not without purpose. They were to accomplish something that would vitally redirect the paths of all humanity. I cannot, nor do I wish to diminish any of the special visitations God has made. There are three distinct visitations that I believe have influenced, and will continue to influence, our modern world more than any other. They are of particular interest to us today. Two of these visits have occurred already, and the other one is set to occur very soon.

First of all, after the divine intervention at the flood judgment of Noah's day, mankind set out again to begin the process of multiplying and replenishing the earth. They were drifting as a nomadic group apparently looking for a place to settle down. Eventually, they came into a beautiful, well fertilized and well watered valley. There they decided they had everything they would ever need so they settled and it became their home. This decision began a phase in scripture that would expose the dark nature of Satan as revealed in the human creature. In this early episode, what we have learned about humanity has continued to reveal itself throughout human history. Through this early event, we can learn many significant truths about how God desires for us to live together as a community of humanity.

To help us understand the significance of this first divine intervention, we should try to understand the concept of home, from the divine perspective. To us, home is the place where we can plant our roots and build our life. It is where we find safety and peace in what may sometimes be an unusually cruel and cold world. In most cases, our most cherished life memories have something to do with home and family. The question coming to surface is this, does our definition of home fit God's definition, and His expectation of what home should be? I think the answer may surprise most people.

Absolutely, home is the place God has in mind as the place from which to launch our lives. However, He has never expected us to drive our stakes in so deeply that we cannot move when He beckons, if He beckons. The writer of Hebrews referred to father Abraham after He answered the call of God on his life, ".....for he waited for a city which has foundations, whose builder and maker is God". (Hebrews 11:10 NKJV) Residing in the place God has chosen for us, in essence, is the divine perspective of home. It is the reason the scene at Babel was especially troubling to the Almighty. God gave us home as a secure bastion on earth, but He never wants us to lose sight of the fact that or earthly home is only temporary.

So why would this be the case? To find the answer, we should examine the text that outlines the motives of these first nomads. Motives are a very important concept when trying to understand why the actions of Noah's descendants led them to a divine intervention. When we read back in the beginning at creation, we are reminded that God's original will for humanity was that we multiply, fill, and subdue the earth. This divine expectation has never changed!

It seems as though these early wanderers briefly forgot this when they came into the beautiful and lush valley of Shinar. Instead, they began to scheme about how they could build a name for themselves, "Let us make a name for ourselves, lest we be scattered abroad over the face of the earth." This was their stated purpose according to Genesis. "Come, let us build ourselves a city, and tower whose top will reach into the heavens" was their battle cry. (Do these aspirations to build, bring anything to mind when we think of our modern world?.....For instance, the World Trade center and what is now the Freedom Tower. It makes me wonder, from what is it we are trying to free ourselves?) Suddenly, their lives became all about themselves. To pursue their selfish desires became their priority. Sadly, this seems to be our mindset today. It seems that doing the will of God was no longer their priority, nor ours. They acted on the most base of human and satanic of impulses. They wanted to be like God, by making gods of themselves. They were guilty just as Eve was in the beginning when succumbing to the serpent in the garden.

It can be said, their motives were to build themselves a name and exalt themselves before God and the masses. Instead of subduing the earth, they now turned to the attempt of subduing each other. The same spirit was seen in the rise of many communist nations throughout history where some of the most atrocious acts against humanity occurred. The leaders of these nations have proven the heinous dark nature and horrific acts that can dwell in the mind of people as they prowl for power and control. Those who lust for power are never satisfied. It seems as if establishing and exercising control over other human beings is the ultimate power "fix" for them.

Today, we are witnessing the resurgence of this spiritually wicked governmental philosophy here in America. It has never gone away. It is the ultimate enemy of individual liberty, personal responsibility, and accountability. These are three of the key scriptural concepts that our nation was founded upon. Unfortunately, these three concepts may soon disappear from our western mindset unless the hideous doctrines of political correctness are destroyed.

The "hold outs" who still believe in these values are finding themselves the targets of those who refuse to accept sound biblical doctrine and common sense morality. The demonic enemies of the cross continue to find their voice within the halls of the White House, Court House, and the House of Representatives. They are using their voice to try to undermine and silence the works of righteousness that has been, and can be again, achieved through Christ.

Unfortunately, for those of us here in America, we have never been closer to adopting the demonic philosophy of socialism ourselves. Even in religious circles, we are witnessing this perversion. Many religious leaders are frantically trying to build a following to enable them to move and manipulate the masses, some for good, but many with vile and satanic motives. Many are changing, or are attempting to change, the message of God to something more politically acceptable by distorting the clear message of scripture. God's people must discern the difference in these who are actually wicked imposters and those who are truly engaged in the building of the kingdom of God. "You will know them by their fruits." (Mat. 7:16 NKJV)

Constructing large buildings and attracting large crowds who pay their tithes is not our divine purpose, contrary to the doctrine of these imposters. I wonder what our reply will be when Jesus ask why we had the air conditioned square footage in the church building yet we allowed multitudes to sleep in the streets in the heat and the cold. Why did we take all this wealth and spend it making ourselves comfortable? Instead of being one unified body, why did we spend our time competing with each other and tearing each other down? These and many other issues have weakened us and gave Satan the foothold he needs to wreak havoc within our world.

Today, the core philosophy of our government is more government control and less individual freedom. We are witnessing the erosion of our basic rights, as outlined by our founding fathers, having designed our government to reflect the Judeo-Christian morality and integrity. The motives of the early founders had nothing to do with politics. The founders fought for a just and safe society. The Democratic Party has basically affirmed a new progressive and unholy ideology and goal. The belief is that government should be our answer for every social ill, even for those ills they themselves have created or fabricated to fit their agenda. Even if it is a bad savior, they want a populace dependent upon the state and who are ignorant to the many atrocities taking place within it. It is their belief that government knows best and should control as much of our lives as possible.

The Republicans claim to vehemently disagree with this doctrine but only do so in order to appease their voter base. They would never state it publicly, but they do seem to silently condone this philosophy of government control while reaping the benefits from special interest. They no longer have the interest of the common people at heart. The problem of special interest is both a democratic and republican issue. In the end, the common person has no voice. They seem to have very little courage to actually do the right thing. This comes at a high price to the American people. We are finding our personal values and our desires for justice and liberty, in practice, are not at all the priorities of our elected officials. It is an extremely sad condition for a so-called "Christian Nation." We were warned about this condition by the founding fathers.

We have bestowed vast amounts of power and trust in individuals who, in many cases, have traded their personal integrity for corruption. This comes at a great cost to those of us who still hunger for a just and righteous society. The "powerful few" control the insignificant and powerless many. This seems to be the political goal of the day. No one in their right minds can argue to the contrary.

Our governmental philosophy has changed. It has become satanic and is in direct contradiction to the divine will of the Creator. It is the "beginning of the end" as humanity is frantically trying to resurrect the "Babel Project" and establish a global power structure with one head. God will not allow this wickedness to prevail for much longer and especially in America. Our founding fathers specifically, and emphatically, dedicated this country to God's purposes and His divine will. We may have forgotten this but God never will! He will act as he did in Babel. Read the book of Revelation. The message is becoming perfectly clear every new day, and we are very close to seeing its reality!

So what exactly did God do in Babel? It was really ingenious (of course I suppose we should expect no less, duh, it is God)! God established Himself as an anti-progressive by confusing the languages of those gathered there. He effectively divided the community of humanity by dividing the language. They could not understand each other, therefore they could not work together.

I might mention, this is one of very few times where God has actually been a divider of people. His message is typically one of unity and love. At least, this is the message of these latter days through Christ. Division was necessary to protect the defenseless from the evils being imagined against them by those whose only goal was to become lords over the people.

According to Genesis chapter ten, God's actions were effectively the birthing of the nations. From this point, they went different ways. Unfortunately, His divine action set the stage for all the animosities that would develop, throughout history, between the nations. It was the seed of all the great wars we have known since that moment in history. His action did postpone the advancement of humanism and all the evils that come along with it. It delayed the goal of establishing a one world governmental order by more than forty centuries. Ultimately, it sets the stage for a coming world chaos and the judgment of the nations by the Almighty. The book of Revelations describes this pending judgment in detail.

The long term effects of this first chapter of human history are misunderstood at best. This chapter of our history was incredibly important in establishing the eventual work of salvation through Christ. It was also incredibly important in establishing the groundwork for the "second" great intervention which occurred about two thousand years later. This next intervention would provide humanity a way to break through the language barrier once again. This second intervention is greatly misunderstood and misinterpreted. For all who would receive it, it would provide a way to reunite all peoples under the banner of God!

A Holy Ghost Filled Messiah
Reuniting the Nations

After two thousand years of war, squabbling, religious manipulation, and religious perversions.....God acted again. This time, He acted just as decisively and effectively as He had at Babel. God's motive this time was not to divide humanity, but it was to reunite them under the banner of holiness. To accomplish this mammoth task, He imparted the gifts to humanity addressed in the previous chapter. This chapter is about the results of these gifts and their impact to the nations.

Of particular interest to us, in the context of this chapter, is the gift of tongues. Through Him the record was set straight.....once and for all. He was completing His work as the messiah, the sacrificial Lamb of God. He gave us the second gift, the Holy Spirit. The Spirit was the one who would impart spiritual gifts on all those who would receive God's work of holiness.

The gift of tongues was the very first manifestation of the Holy Spirit when He descended upon the believers on the day of Pentecost. This is significant, as it marks the first time since Babel that a man could speak and be understood by all nationalities and in their native language. What a divine interpreter! The foreigners who were in town for the Holy Day of the Jewish Shavuot, the feast of weeks which occurred fifty days after Passover, were witnesses and participants of this event. In this case, it was also fifty days after Passover and the crucifixion of our Savior.

> (Acts 2:8—12 NKJV) "8 And how is it that we hear, each in our own language in which we were born? 9 Parthians and Medes and Elamites, those dwelling in Mesopotamia, Judea and Cappadocia, Pontus and Asia, 10 Phrygia and Pamphylia, Egypt and the parts of Libya adjoining Cyrene, visitors from Rome, both Jews and proselytes, 11 Cretans and Arabs — we hear them speaking in our own tongues the wonderful works of God." 12 So they were all amazed and perplexed, saying to one another, "Whatever could this mean?"

I believe the gift of tongues may be one of the most misinterpreted, and therefore the most misapplied, of all the special gifts. Based on the evidence as reported in the book of Acts, the believers, at the final instruction of Jesus were in the upper room waiting. Waiting on what? They were waiting for the power from on high that Jesus had promised them. They were waiting for a divine act of God. Something supernatural! They were powerless to accomplish this on their own. The scripture tells us that the Spirit came suddenly and as a mighty rushing wind. Immediately, those that were gathered there began to speak with other tongues. For those who spoke and for those who heard, this miracle was two-fold and very significant.

What a surprise it must have been, just as it was the first nomads who awakened unable to understand a word spoken by a large portion of those in their tribe. This time, the Word came forth from a small band of believers who had not been trained in their language, yet they understood. First of all, the miracle occurred in those who spoke. The Holy Spirit took control of their tongues. I believe that those who spoke were speaking exactly as they always had, yet what was coming out was something they had never experienced or prepared for. God divinely translated the words from their mouths to the ears of those who were in the city.

The Holy Spirit took their native tongue and translated it into the languages of everyone present. For the first time since the Babel intervention, humanity now had the opportunity to be reunited and understand each other once again. How awesome is that? A new and heavenly language had come. All of this came through the presence of the indwelling Holy Spirit of God.

However, they were not left to their own evil impulses that would drive them to lord over one another. This time, they would be filled with the Word of God, as delivered by Jesus and the Holy Spirit, who would communicate to them the desire of Almighty God. He would motivate them to love and care for one another in a way mankind had never experienced. This Holy Spirit would empower them to eliminate the fleshly impulses that could cause them to bring one another under subjection and bondage. This is the first breath of the church.

From that day forward, this overcoming power became the essence of the "Church". It always has been, and it always will be! Anyone who is not experiencing this overcoming power today is simply plugged into the wrong power source and is living a carnal religion. Salvation will happen by the Word. It is enabled by the Holy Spirit who is present in the life of every true believer. There is no other entity that can accomplish this end. There is no need for one!

I am ashamed to confess, for a large portion of my life, I have not really understood the damage that one simple act of rebellion can cause. I witness pure evil becoming more and more prevalent in our American culture, and it has caused me to stop and re-evaluate the decisions I have made throughout my life. Have I helped others to see the light of blessing through simple faith and obedience? Have I been a good example of how a Christian should not be? Am I living a life based on my own preferences and desires?

I know there is a coming day of spiritual reckoning. It will be a terrible day for us all. We will stand before our God without excuse. This is the third and final intervention. He has provided all we will ever need to overcome. Have we squandered it and put our faith and trust in everything else? His judgment is on its way! The horsemen are strapping on their swords and are preparing to mount up! It will be the most terrible day in the history of the earth! It is His last intervention for the age of humanity. He will establish eternal justice and the reign of evil people, along with their warped sense of justice, will be forever terminated. The Master of the house has spoken. He will most certainly accomplish this day of reckoning, and it will involve the fire and brimstone this time!

Chapter Eight

Life's Greatest Miracle, the Long Journey to Salvation, Lessons from the Snow!

Come now, let us reason together, says the Lord:
"Though your sins be as scarlet, they shall be
white as snow; though they be red like crimson,
they shall be as wool." Isaiah 1:18 NKVJ

This past Tuesday, my wife and I received a call from a dear friend, Becky Owens. Becky and her husband Larry had moved away a few years before, and we had not seen them in a while. In fact, the last time my wife had seen them, I was still in the hospital at Memorial. They came to visit. I do not personally remember their visit as this was during my down days! Amazingly, and unfortunately, the call we received this week was to petition prayers as our friend, Larry, had received a tentative diagnoses of pancreatic cancer.

His diagnosis seemed almost identical to my own from over a year and a half ago. My wife and I talked and agreed we should go to Birmingham, to UAB Hospital, where Larry had been admitted. Even though the weather forecast for the next day was a bit scary, we decided to make the trip to Birmingham. Snow and ice was in the forecast throughout our area as far south as Birmingham. We felt that we needed to take the three hour journey to provide whatever support we could, even if it would be a short visit.

We arrived at the hospital and spent several hours, late Tuesday evening and into the early hours of Wednesday morning, conversing with Becky and Larry. Larry was to have a stint placed in his liver on Wednesday morning. We had a sweet time of fellowship with them both. Even though Larry was in obvious discomfort, he still got excited when we started talking scripture and faith and the over-arching plans of God.

How amazing it is to be a witness when someone is in the midst of a trial of faith, yet they joyfully cling to the promises they have accepted. These are the promises they have lived by long before the trials ever came. This is faith in action, faith in reality. There was no pity party to be had here. Larry and Becky both knew beyond a shadow of a doubt they were in the hands of the great healer and His will was their first priority.

The next day we left Birmingham and headed home at about 12:00pm EST. Twenty minutes out of Birmingham, we met up with the beginning of the winter storm. It was a mixture of rain and heavy sleet. We both concluded that God had wanted us to make this trip, and in doing so, He would make a way for us to get home safely. Sure enough, about twenty minutes later, we drove out of all the mess to perfectly dry highways and they remained clear for the remainder of the drive. Almost immediately upon arriving home, at around 5:00pm, the skies opened up and the snow began to fall. It was one of those southern snows, and even though we do not see them very often, we knew it would be serious and would produce heavy snowfall.

Now, fast forward about eight hours! I am sitting in our sunroom, and the outside flood lights are on. I was watching the steady and heavy snowflakes descending from the heavens and laying on our deck and fixtures. By now, six inches had accumulated, and the snow had not relented. I was tired from the stresses of the day and the night before. I was mesmerized by the snow. The scene was surreal!!

I began to think about the snow coming down and why watching it made me feel like a kid again. What is so special about this white stuff that allows it to excite my senses to such a degree? I looked out beyond the porch and could see as the whole world beyond our house had turned a pure white. I thought of a scripture.

> (Ps 51:5—10 NKJV) 5 Behold, I was brought forth in iniquity, and in sin my mother conceived me. 6 Behold, You desire truth in the inward parts, and in the hidden part You will make me to know wisdom. 7 Purge me with hyssop, and I shall be clean; Wash me, and I shall be whiter than snow. 8 Make me hear joy and gladness, that the bones You have broken may rejoice. 9 Hide Your face from my sins, And blot out all my iniquities. 10 Create in me a clean heart, O God, And renew a steadfast spirit within me.

As I thought on this scripture, I began to realize why I have always been so mystified by snow. The answer to my question was becoming clear. The snow was actually painting a portrait of purity for me. I had realized for a moment in time God was covering the drab and the darkness of the earth with His pure whiteness from the heavens. Somehow, the white now settling onto the earth was dispelling some of the darkness. Even though there was no moonlight to be found, the snow was somehow shining through the darkness. For a brief moment in time, God was sculpting a natural picture of His purity and of His desire that His children be pure.

It was a brief picture of the soul of man, of my soul, that has been cleansed by the power of God through the blood of Jesus.

Many of my Christian friends will be wondering what I mean by the title of this chapter. Being a Baptist for all my life, I have certainly not been taught that salvation is a long process. It is a supernatural event taking place instantaneously when a person first puts their faith in Jesus Christ as their Savior. In this chapter, I will be focusing on the fact that true salvation is actually both of these scenarios. In the previous chapter, we discussed two of the gifts (Jesus the Word and the Holy Spirit) God gave us these gifts to reunite the nations under the banner of true holiness. In this chapter, I hope to share how He gave those same gifts to us as individuals to reunite us in true relationship with Him. God enabled us to overcome our own personal sinful potential that sometimes separates us from Him.

I believe as Christians, when we grasp the true nature of spiritual conversion or better said, deliverance, we will realize it is a life-long endeavor that begins with a very bold choice. Realizing this should not distort the true nature of the miracle. It is truly miraculous to see the first seed of faith which creates a spiritual babe and then flourishes into a powerful Christian life. Such a life reveals the divine nature of God to a Godless world. This message of divine provision is one that every Christian should hunger for! In essence it is a "making sense" of the salvation experience.

First of all, this chapter is not only about conversion to Christ. It is about what to do with Him after receiving Him. To be more concise, it is about what He wants to do with us after He receives us. I am afraid we compass land and sea to make converts but then fail miserably at showing and helping them to live in the fullness of their new gift. I am sure that many who are versed in the scriptures remember this charge that Jesus laid upon the Scribes and Pharisees of His day. (See Mat.23:15NKJV)

He went so far as to say that when they make their converts they turn them, "twofold more into a child of hell than they were before." His message was a simple one! He rebuked them for taking so much pain to establish a convert while failing to lead them to the true spiritual gifts. These are the gifts that would have radically changed their lives and made them fit for divine service. This dereliction of duty was not intentional. It was because they had not experienced this personal power of God themselves. This chapter is an effort to confront the doctrine from hell that is deceiving many Christians today. This is a doctrine that is leading believers farther away from God rather than bringing them closer.

One of the greatest needs within the Christian world today is that we come to fully understand what salvation really is *and* what it really is not. The best place to start is in the beginning. In fact, the first definition for salvation is a new beginning. This definition is made most clear by the discussion Jesus had with one of the few temple Rabbis who actually sought out a conversation with Jesus to hear His side of the story. Nicodemus was both amazed and perplexed by the doctrine of Jesus. Specifically, there is one statement Jesus emphatically made during their discourse that aroused the attention of Nicodemus. The statement was, "…..you must be born again". (John 3:7 NKJV)

In my words, "Nicodemus you have got to scrap any preconceived notions you may have. This includes any knowledge that does not fit the truth. It includes any misinterpretations you may have about God up until this very moment in time. You must start all over anew and realize that you have now come to a new place. Through faith, you must accept the real and divine truth about God and life and the life hereafter." This was quite a tall order for one who was an influential temple leader in Israel. If no other examples existed, Nicodemus is proof that religion will never be a sufficient substitute for salvation.

What is this "being born again" thing? How does it happen? It is a valid question! In fact, it was the first question of Nicodemus …..."How can a man be born when he is old?"….. (see John 3:4 NKJV) Jesus responded, "…..You must be born of the water and of the spirit…..". Many have interpreted this to mean that you must be born both physically, the natural birth, and then spiritually…..In other words, from both the womb of a mother and from the womb of the eternal Creator who is spirit. It is only through rebirth that the regeneration of the spirit can occur and we can experience new life.

As human beings, we are fleshly beings who are driven and directed by a spirit, remembering the puppet analogy from earlier. Being born again occurs when we realize that this natural spirit has the potential to drive us farther away from God and His holiness. It is only when we offer the control of our spirit back to the one who gave it to us that we can be spiritually and eternally safe. We should know that the spirit within a human being is divine by nature and now has the potential to reflect either good or evil. The choice that we make concerning Jesus and the truths of God is the factor which determines what our life will produce.

The ultimate spiritual product that we become is determined by the man himself or the woman herself. This is the mystery of "free will!" For many, free will is something with which we often struggle. God will never force Himself or His will upon us. We all start out spiritually neutral, so to speak. If it were not so, God would have preordained blessings for some and cursing for others. We would have had no choice to make! A story was once told about a Rabbi who taught….. "Inside of every man there lived two dogs, a white one and a black one. These two dogs fought all the time." When asked which one would win, the Rabbi stated, "The one we feed the most." Salvation is our willful return to the Creator, through Jesus, to make Him the divine kennel keeper of our life and of our spirit. Only God can provide the food that can cleanse our soul from the blackness of sin and will make the "white dog" strong enough to dominate all other forces in our lives.

The salvation experience is a deliberate return to God through faith and humility. When we choose to allow Him to change us, He will. After this, He will make of us something fit for His service and kingdom. In essence, true salvation is to reject ourselves with all of our self-dependency and sufficiency. If we effectively do this, we become like a new baby. God encloses our spirit and soul within His care and seals it until the day of redemption. (Eph. 4:30 KJV) We cannot possibly know all the things God has planned for us when we are first born again. We must learn to be willing to receive His plans as He presents them.

This truth sets the stage for many conflicts between "Our Will" and His "Divine Will!" We must allow His "Divine Will" to prevail if we are to live in victory and power. Everything we know must be re-learned through the lens of our Creator Father and His Son Jesus Christ. There are no divisions or disagreements between the two of them. Fortunately for us, we are not left on our own to accomplish this amazing transition. In fact, it is impossible for us to make the transition on our own!

In sum, these paragraphs define the basic steps every person must take, through faith, in order to be born again. The steps to true salvation involve personal submission, confession, and reception. Salvation will not be gained by demanding it. It is through humbly petitioning the Father, in repentance as an unworthy vessel that we are saved. It cannot be attained by setting conditions of what we are willing to give up and what we are not. True salvation can only come when we are willing to surrender it all and start over. We must be willing to receive it in all its fullness. Contrary to liberal and modern interpretations, it only comes through one source, the Lord Jesus Christ. If anyone tries to attain salvation in any other way, they are the same as a thief or robber, and a rebellious rejecter of the truth. (John 10:1 NKJV) Yes, this is closed minded, but it is the only way home. The Father has made the ultimate sacrifice in providing us His perfect Son. He has interpreted the truth for us and has revealed the violently evil nature existing in us all! After the cross, He will never compromise, and God have mercy on us if we do!

If you are fortunate enough to find a Christian friend or church that is bold enough to tell you the truth about sin and your sinful nature, your first action should be to come to Jesus. If you come fully seeking it, complete forgiveness and everlasting life and fellowship await you. After conversion, many well-meaning Christians will encourage you to come and join their fellowship. They desire to teach you about what it means to be a Christian.

I would encourage you to join with a fellowship of Christian believers. Start blooming where you believe God has planted you. I would be remiss if I did not first forewarn you about some of the common pitfalls you may encounter. Church membership is important for learning and growth but not all churches are focused on your growth and development. The most important responsibility of any Christian is to establish a relationship with God. The most important role of any church is to help you do that. To do this is in no way an overnight process. It will involve hurt and heartache as you grow to be what God ultimately wants you to become. What I have shared with you is something I have wished many times someone would have shared with me when I was first saved. It would have saved me a ton of heartaches, disappointments, and even deceptions if I had only known.

You will find that these gifts are all sufficient to accomplish the divine purposes of God in your life. They are sufficient from the day you are born again, until the day you leave this earth to be in God's presence. The entire purpose of the church, from a stewardship perspective, is to make sure you are introduced and taught the essential gifts. They will lead you to victory over your desire to sin. The Church is to provide guidance on how to recognize the spiritual landmines in your life and then diffuse them using the Word and the Spirit, by coupling them with the third gift, prayer! If the church you are attending does not actively educate and train you in these three things, you need to be looking for a church that will.

Do not be fooled into thinking that merely following some prescribed format of religious programming will accomplish the deliverance that God has in mind for you. You can never hope to experience the fullness of your salvation until you can learn to apply these gifts in your own life in a personal way. They were provided because they are absolutely necessary for accomplishing complete and total recognition and deliverance from personal sin. Receiving these gifts and learning to use them will put you on a direct pathway to the throne room of God. There are still plenty of churches that believe in the unadulterated Word, the power of the Holy Spirit, and effectual Prayer. They are not as easy to find as in times past.

The gift of prayer should be used to provide a way to determine what church membership should look like for you. It is not a strong evangelical outreach. It is not religious works of any kind, done to somehow appease or make God happy. It is not paying your tithe and giving offerings to the poor. Prayer is the beginning of your faith and will help you to experience all of these in the way God has planned. It is not experiencing miracles that leave you amazed. These things are all bi-products of your faith. These things all have their place, but they are not the source or the means of your salvation. Instead, they are the end or the evidence of your salvation.

Effective prayer must be accompanied by a love for and a dependence upon the Word of God. It must be linked to a personal relationship with the Holy Spirit. The Spirit is your inspiration and guide to the truths within the Word. The Word will guide you in how you should pray. The scripture says, "The effectual fervent prayer of a righteous man avails much!" Without the Word and without the Holy Spirit, there will be no righteousness. In other words, your prayers will be powerless without the presence of these two gifts in your life.

They work in concert with one another to create within you a formidable opponent to the sin nature which battles for dominance. They will provide the power to defeat the satanic influences which constantly contend for control. These three gifts, when brought into alignment in your life, will provide all you will ever need to achieve full and complete deliverance. They will be a shield against the sins attempting to assault and vex your righteous soul. As these three gifts are implemented in your life, you will find the power to carry your faith to the world. As a human being, you are still an imperfect creature, but your motives will be guided by the divine. You are now in a position to fully experience God in ways unimaginable!

Chapter Nine

Family, Reflections, and Revelations

**Our family, together for our "Gathering of Angels."
Celebrating the one year anniversary of our brand new
life after the "code". A day of golf and great food.**

**My beautiful bride at the beginning of our Thanksgiving
holiday, 2013. Smoky Mountains bound. But
first, a stop in Knoxville to see the Eagles.**

A View from a Wife.....On the Outside Looking In

I recount our story, from time to time, for those who may have heard about it and are curious about the "details." Every time I talk about it, I usually end up in tears. The tears still come from that place of sorrow to blessing. I believe God will only trust certain people with certain things because He knows they will use it to glorify Him. I believe my husband was one of those people. God trusted my husband. It is now that I will tell our difficult but sweet story and yes, most certainly with tears.

As I write for this book, I have been a nurse for 30 years. The majority of that time I have been an L&D nurse. My time as a nurse is spent, on the whole, in a wonderful exciting environment. What could be more awesome than seeing a new, sweet, tiny baby enter this world? I absolutely love the field of medicine. The day my husband came home with the news of his potential medical condition, while accepting the news as a nurse, I was first and foremost a wife.....a wife very much in love with this man. I believe

Tony and I have experienced a love that a great many people miss in life. To this point, I had not considered a life without my love. We usually do not entertain the idea of not having one another.

When Tony came home that day, after having the ultrasound at Dr. Swan's office, the wife and not the nurse responded to the news. I thought Tony was having gallbladder issues. As Tony has recounted before, and as I can still see so plainly today, he entered the kitchen where I had prepared dinner. He was trying to be upbeat, but his words struck my soul. Tony's words, "We may have a battle on our hands. It is not the gallbladder it is a mass on my pancreas." My poor husband was not very comforted by me. All I could do was cry, and cry, and cry. I cried all the way to bedtime. I would awaken, from light sleep, with so much sorrow and I would start crying again. This potential problem had engulfed me. I could not wait for the morning. We had a CT scheduled at the hospital where I presently work and have since September 1986. The CT would help us to know more about this "mass" on the pancreas.

We had not spoken with anyone since Tony came home with the news. I needed someone to talk to and people to pray. While Tony was getting ready, I went next door to my parent's house before we were to leave for the hospital. It was a very warm beautiful morning. We sat out back by their pool and yes, I started crying again. Through all of the tears I explained to my mom and dad what we might be up against. They were very supportive with their love. Being believers, mom and dad (Roy and Catherine Rollins) started the prayer chain.

We arrived at the hospital. Tony checked in and medical personnel were preparing him for the CT. I went to see my hospital family, my L&D sisters. They were all wonderful and supportive with hugs, their own tears, and encouragement of prayers. As we stood there, Wanda Perry, ACNO, came through and just at the right time. She walked with me to radiology and spoke with Dr. Brent Barrow on our behalf. Dr. Barrow, a Radiologist, read Tony's scan, and He gave us the tentative report. The best part of the report was that it appeared there was no metastasis. Now, in reporting that, it did appear there was an issue of great concern. We were redirected to Dr. Swan and he further directed us to surgical oncology. That is where we met Dr. Charles Portera Jr., a surgical oncologist at Memorial hospital in Chattanooga, Tn.

**(L-R) Gina Frederick, Barbara Dickerson,
Beverly Dunn, and Suzanne Bynum.**

I was investigating all avenues and we were also scheduled to meet with physicians at Johns Hopkins. We had settled on the potential diagnosis of "pancreatic cancer." We were praying fervently, and many others were holding the line in prayer with us. As Tony has recounted, after our appointment with Dr. Portera, arrangements were made for further testing. Dr. Gregory Olds performed an endoscopic ultrasound at Memorial. Our diagnosis was confirmed. Tony would have to undergo a major surgery called a "Whipple procedure", and we wanted to move on it as quickly as possible. Tony was immediately drawn to Dr. Portera and wanted him to perform the surgery. We had spoken to others and mentioned Dr. Portera. He was extremely well thought of for his surgical skill, and he had performed a number of these specialty procedures. We both agreed on Dr. Portera, and we then canceled the appointment at Johns Hopkins. The surgery date was scheduled, August 27, 2013.

We had shared our news with everyone so that prayers would be flowing. Our heavenly Father was, and is, so wonderful to sweetly encourage us on. Tony and I had prayed and sought the Word. The day before Tony went in for surgery, this scripture came to me. I posted it to social media, "Be still and know that I am God….."(Psalms 46:10 NKJV) My scripture for the day of surgery was as follows, "The Lord will fight for you and you shall hold your peace." (Exodus 14:14 NKJV) And fight He did!

The last time I had heard the words, "Whipple procedure," was in nursing school. I remembered the content of what the procedure entailed, but I had not known of anyone who had the procedure done. To give you a short overview of the procedure, it includes the removal of the part of the pancreas involved, removal of one third of the stomach, a portion of the small intestine and the gallbladder. Tony's surgery was five and one half hours in duration. Dr. Portera came and spoke with us and reported that the procedure had gone well, but they were working to get his pain under control. He would then be moved to ICU where he would stay for 48 to 72 hours. We would be able to see him in ICU after he was settled.

After a few hours, Tony was moved from recovery to ICU. After another hour or two, Justin and I got to go in and see him. I was not expecting to see Tony the way he was as Justin and I walked into his ICU room. He was sitting up in a chair and eating ice. What a wonderful site! His nurse was Brian Sax, RN, and we discussed Tony's recovery and of course golf…..This is how the words, "golf saved my life," became a teasing catch phrase for us.

Social Media-Legacy of Prayer and Faith:

Posted by: Beverly Rollins Dunn – Sept. 15th, 2013 Chattanooga, Tn.

Well, day number 19 in the hospital with my sweet husband. Tony is doing great, by the grace of God. He has been dismissed from care by his nephrologist, acute care physician, and PT. Tomorrow is his fifth day on Coumadin per protocol. Please pray that his INR levels are within range. He walked around MICU twice today and is continuing to increase his diet intake. His drains are clear. Thank you all for continued prayer. Our love and praise to God our Father.

The surgery had been wonderfully successful, and it appeared that our recovery was going to be just as great. Tony was way ahead of schedule and was moved to a regular room, on the fifth floor, the very next afternoon. This was not the typical ICU recovery time for a Whipple procedure. We were told to expect an ICU stay of forty-eight to eventy-two hours. During the next nine days, our home was the fifth floor with our wonderful angel staff. A few years before, Tony had been diagnosed with a DVT (Deep Vein Thrombosis). After the Whipple procedure, he was placed on Heparin injections twice daily as a preventative treatment.

Social Media-Legacy of Prayer and Faith:

Posted by: Beverly Rollins Dunn – Sept. 19ᵗʰ, 2013 Chattanooga, Tn.

This is Day 23 of our amazing journey. Tony is progressing wonderfully. He walked out of MICU last night to make a round through the courtyard and down the hall. (Got to see where the family has been living.) We are projected to go home Saturday. His blood work has to be in order, with an INR of 3.0 (2.8 this morning), and stay elevated above 2 for 24 hours after they stop the blood thinner drip. He is eating small amounts of regular diet without problems. Thanking and praising Jehovah Rapha, the Lord our healer.

It was ten days post op and we were ready to head back to our home in the valley. Everything was great with Tony's recovery. He had an occasional blockage of his stomach tube, but otherwise, everything was on schedule. We had developed our routine from the very first day on the fifth floor. We were up for breakfast, then a walk around the halls, then a bath and sitting or walking or visiting. The day we were to go home was no different. Tony and I were waiting for Dr. Portera's nurse, Deanna Hopkins, to come check on us and order his discharge home. We decided to get his bath before leaving. Deanna had a meeting that morning. She had been reminded by her office staff. This meeting delayed her from her usual rounding time. Deanna's meeting, unbeknownst to us, would be a blessing. Tony had a large abdominal incision from this major surgery and he had a tube in his stomach for feedings. Due to the stomach and feeding tubes, I assisted him daily with bed baths. Tony wanted to be up to the bathroom first, and then I would help with his bath. This was our daily routine. Today would prove to be anything but "routine." The scripture verse I had posted to social media the previous night, Sept. 5, 2013, "…To give them beauty for ashes, the oil of joy for mourning. The garment of praise for the spirit of heaviness; They will be called trees of righteousness, a planting of the Lord that He may be glorified." (Isaiah 61:3 NKJV). I thought God was talking to us about the successful surgery. Little did I know God had planned something far more magnificent to show us!

Nurse Deanna with Bev and me at the
"Gathering of Angels" Celebration

When Tony came back from the bathroom, he went straight to the bedside chair and said, "I feel like I cannot catch my breath." "I am having trouble breathing." I still remember his face and those struggling words. The nurse/wife in me knew we were not going home that day, and I immediately hit the nurse call button to get help. I knew immediately it was most likely a pulmonary embolism. These are two really big words for a "clot in the lungs." Little did I know how big those two words would prove to be. His nurse that day, Mariamma, followed by a multitude of medical personnel and equipment, came flowing into the room. Tony was placed on his bed and hooked up to monitors. There was a flurry of activity as people came in and out of the room. The excitement was almost palpable. They looked concerned but moved and aided Tony proficiently. They were a well-oiled machine. I cannot say enough about our angel staff....... Breathing was a great effort for Tony and he was pale, cool, and clammy. We kept making eye contact, and I was trying to smile. I wanted to reassure him, and it was all I could do to hold back my tears. He looked a little rattled by it all, and I was going to be supportive. He was taken swiftly to CT for conformation of what I am sure everyone was thinking. I was told he would be taken to CT and then straight to ICU. That is exactly what happened. I was to wait in his room for further instructions.

Holly Vandergriend fifth floor nurse helped lead the emergency response at the onset of the code.

**Some of our fifth floor caregivers.
From left to right, Ruth Lightsey, Amber Forster Simpson,
Bev Dunn, Tony Dunn, and Mariamma Varghese.**

I cried after Tony left. The nursing supervisor of the fifth floor, Brooke Kelly, asked one of her staff nurses to pray with me. Sweet little AJ prayed with me outside of Tony's room. My thoughts were still fairly positive. I was thinking, "He will be placed on a Heparin drip to clear the clots and he will be fine".….optimistic last thoughts.

I immediately phoned my mom and dad, and they were in route to the hospital. I phoned Justin, followed by Tara and her fiancé Mike. I felt that Mike would be Tara's strong supporter, and I was right. I phoned our friends Rick and Marilyn Gibson. They had been close to us through this whole ordeal and so supportive with prayer. I knew they would get the prayer chain moving.

As planned, Tony was taken directly from CT to ICU. Justin had now arrived at the hospital. When they had Tony somewhat settled, they let Justin and I go in to see him. The head of the bed was up, and Tony had a breathing mask completely covering his face. The mask is called a BIPAP mask. He appeared to be struggling so much to breath. His ICU nurse was Alison Patterson, R.N. She was a very sweet and calm nurse. We met the attending doctor, Dr. Steciw. Dr. Steciw was watching the monitor above Tony's head and I heard her ask Alison if an "Echo" had been done. I could tell by her expression that things were very serious, and we were asked to leave the room. I am sure Tony was trying to encourage Justin and Me. All Tony could do was give us a "thumbs up" sign.

Nurse Alison Patterson, MICU

We exited his room and went back to the ICU waiting room where two of Justin's coworker friends, my mom and dad, and Marilyn and Rick Gibson had arrived. We were sitting there talking and within a few minutes the cardiac ACNP, Neely Cotton, came out and told us that Tony was still having trouble and they would be starting a Heparin drip. Great, I thought, we are on our way to solving this issue! Neely had reappeared a few minutes later and said they were not going to start Heparin but use a different drug. OK, I thought, things will turn around with something better. Neely came back after another 10 minutes with Dr. Brooke Daniel, a Hematologist / Oncologist. This was the first time we had met Dr. Daniel. She discussed the use of another medication that they may want to try.

We were grateful for the updates that came so quickly. Neely came out again and told us that Tony was really struggling to breathe, and he was not doing well. They had to change the plan of care again. Tony's condition had declined rapidly, and the decision was made to inject the big drug, TPA, a clot buster. To do this procedure, he would need to be taken to radiology. At this point, my heart was beginning to sink. I had asked if we could see him before he was taken to radiology. Neely escorted us to a little nook by the ICU doors. She told us to wait there and we would get a quick glimpse of Tony as he came by. Justin and I sat and talked as we waited for him to pass through…..and waited…..and waited. Neely came to the little nook after a long wait and said they had no choice but to do the TPA in Tony's ICU room because he had been too unstable and was rapidly declining. She followed this by saying, "Tony's heart has stopped now and they are "coding" him (CPR) and you just need to pray."

This is where the tears begin as that day comes back into view. I remember completely losing control. I can still hear, as I did that day, what seemed to be the moaning of someone else. It was not someone else, it was me. The sorrowful moans came from the absolute depths of my soul and was overpowering. Justin and I left the nook and walked back to the waiting room where everyone else had gathered. I felt as if I could hardly stand. Family and friends had come to be with us and had gathered around for prayer. Terry Rollins, my cousin, led us I prayer. He happened to be close by and had received word about Tony. It was so mournful that they moved us to a private family waiting room just outside of the ICU. We would wait there for further news.

I can remember rocking back and forth as I sat on a two-person chair. I cried to God, "please, please, please." This seemed to be the only word I could manage, but I was confident that my intercessor was carrying the words of my heart to God. My mom sat with me, and with her arms around me and her head lowered to mine, she kept saying, "you have got to believe." I remember saying, "I do" but I could only mourn out loud. This mourning came from the depths of my being and out. It was as if I was on the outside looking in. It was at this point that my mother called us to prayer. To this day, I cannot even remember the words.

By this time, family and friends were getting the news and were arriving to be with us. Oh what a great comfort they were. The little room we occupied was packed wall to wall. Our supporters included my brother, Eddie Rollins and his wife Misty and my two nephews, Cory and Connor Rollins. Justin's wife Amanda had arrived. After hearing the news, Amanda's parents, Jerry and Norma Calaway had come from their home in North Carolina. Jerry brought Amanda to the hospital while Norma cared for Justin and Amanda's children, our grandchildren, at their home. There was a multiple of family and friends. Tara and Mike were en route from Knoxville, and I remember thinking about the sadness for Justin and Tara. Tony's dad and some of his siblings had arrived and I remember the sadness I felt for them. The little family room was overflowing with people. The hospital chaplain came to join us and pray with us. I can still see his kind, sweet face. He sat with us for a long time and encouraged us with the Word of God. I believe he received an extra jewel in his crown that day as the person occupying the chair beside him was my dad. Those who understand my dad's tendency to be a "talker," understand what I mean.

There were three ICU physicians that I remember meeting. I had met Dr. Steciw in Tony's ICU room before he coded, and she was on it! One physician I can remember seeing, Dr. Pesce, but I believe I met him after the code. The third physician I remember vividly, Dr.Baleeiro. Neely came to the family room with Dr. Baleeiro, while the code was still in progress, and had been for what I would estimate to be twenty-five to thirty minutes. I stood up to talk to him when he entered the room and he said, "Things do not look good and he is not responding to anything we are doing." His face is still very clear in my memory and especially as I responded to him. I felt an overwhelming need to talk to Tony, even though I knew he would be intubated and unable to speak. I was hopeful he could listen (those that know me well know that I am a talker). I asked Dr. Baleeiro if I could see Tony, "I need to talk to him." I simply cannot describe the urgency I felt. I am pretty sure he did not expect that request because I remember the look on his face. He paused and then said, "Well you know we are still working on him?" I acknowledged his comment and he then said, "Give us about five minutes to get some things arranged and someone will come and get you."

When reflecting back on this, I have wondered if Dr. Baleeiro thought I would give an indication as to halting their efforts, in part because he thought Tony was going to die or had died already......why not let me visit this last time. At the time, these things had not even occurred to me. I just needed to see Tony and talk to him! I had asked Justin if he wanted to go with me. I reassured Justin that he did not have to go, but I had to see his dad. He agreed that he wanted to go and after a few minutes, they came back to get us.

The curtain was closed to the ICU room where Tony was being coded. You could hear activity. As they led us in, I do not remember seeing lots of people or equipment, although I know that both were there. The first thing that caught my eye was Tony's stomach tube hanging from his side. The tube was moving as they were doing chest compressions. I remember seeing a man doing chest compressions. Later, I would find that man to be such a wonderful part of our story, ICU nurse, Bill Bolton, RN. As I looked to the head of the bed, I immediately made my way up to see Tony's face. His eyes were open and had the fixed and "glazed over" look. As a nurse, I had seen this empty look before. Tony's eyes appeared as those from someone that had passed. My heart sank. All I could remember to do was to talk to him, as if he would actually be able to listen. I got close to his ear and as I continued to look at his face, I could only ask him not to leave. The words came, "please don't leave." I had not noticed where Justin was but he had stayed at the back of the room. As Justin was praying, and as I was making a spoken request, a holy communion was taking place as a witness in that room. After seeing Tony, the mourning began to rise more than ever. As Justin and I left the ICU room, I was so very thankful to have the aid of

Justin to assist me out. I thought it would be the last time I would see my husband "alive." My urgency to get to Tony was also driven by the idea of, "I do not want him to be alone....."

We returned to our family room that was now overflowing with people. My heart was broken. There are certain things I can remember distinctly, but some are a blur. After a very long time of "coding" my husband, (we found out much later the total duration of the code was 55 minutes) Dr. Portera came into the family room where we were all gathered. I will never forget this. He came to sit beside me in the corner of that little room. He had such a strange, almost questioning look on his face. His words to me, "We have a heartbeat." "You have hope." Later, we were told that Dr. Portera had been in Tony's ICU room, during the code, while Justin and I were there. I had not seen him there as my vision was so fixed on my husband. Dr. Portera had attempted to come to our family waiting room and speak to us. Later, he told us there was so much sorrow coming from that room and he could not come in. We had also been told that Dr. Portera had been asked if he wanted to "call the code." He did not answer them.

Dr. Portera sat in the corner of that little room with my family. He explained to me his encounter with Tony from a few minutes earlier. The code was over and Tony had a heartbeat. Dr. Portera's main concern was that even though Tony had a heartbeat, what brain activity might have been lost and the possibility he would be in a vegetative state. After all, Tony had been coded for fifty-five minutes. In evaluating Tony, to see what the impact to the brain had been, Dr. Portera performed a "sternal rub." In doing so, you take the knuckles of one hand and rub the breastbone of the person. If brain damage had occurred there would be a certain activity, or reflex, from the rub. This procedure would indicate whether it was a reflex or if the person would respond with an intact Central Nervous System. The response was not a reflex. Tony was aware. The sternal rub is not comfortable. Tony's response was one of discomfort. To make sure he was seeing the response correctly, Dr. Portera reported he did this a second time and then a third time. I remember Dr. Portera's look of bewilderment and his words, "So I did it again." I remember a little chuckle as I said, "well by the third time you were probably just ticking him off." Dr. Portera restated, "We have a long way to go, but you have hope." Yes we did!

We did hope! Prayers were sent out with the specific things we needed to happen. We prayed to the Father believing that He who started a good work in Tony would see it through. God answered so sweetly….. The first visit after the code, the kids and I went in to see Tony. He was on a ventilator and he had eight out of nine IV pumps running. His nurse at the beginning of this ordeal was still his nurse after, Alison. When we entered the room she stated, "This man must still have something to say." "God is not through with him yet." There was a red "crash cart" in the room and Alison said, "We used three of these on him." When Justin nodded in approval, she was even more expressive and waved her hands over the cart and said, "You don't understand. We used three of these." There was also a younger nurse with Alison. She came and stood at the entrance to Tony's room. She had a sweet smile on her face and just stood there. When she spoke, it was to comment on the unbelief of the situation that she had just witnessed. She made a comment, in reference to Justin and I coming into the Tony's ICU room during the code, and she recounted that I had asked Tony not to leave.

From this point forward, Justin would lead us in prayer at each ICU visit over the next several days. The visits were at least four times a day. Justin would close the prayer for us, "we pray that you would heal dad from the top of his head to the bottom of his feet!" I love this and will always remember it. For days, there were new adventures in our journey. Our God supplied all of Tony's needs and our needs. Tony had responded amazingly, even though he was on a ventilator. We would talk and Tony would raise an eyebrow or have the look of a frown on his face. He would attempt to communicate with us. At one point, he made hand gestures that he wanted to write. The nurse that provided the paper and pencil told us not to be surprised if the writing did not work, and his writing would probably be scribble. He was still under partial sedation because of being on the ventilator.

As he placed pencil to paper, he wrote. It was difficult to read at times but at other times very legible. We had learned that you had to move the paper as he wrote or the writing was bunched in one spot. His rings bothered him because of the swelling of his hands. After surgery, he wanted to put his rings on, and his rings were on when he coded. He wrote "rings" in big letters and we removed them. We would question and he would write. His answers were at times witty. I had asked him a specific question, "Do you know what happened to you?" Tony's written response to this question and correctly spelled was "Pulmonary Embolism." Even on a ventilator, the long words that I had made reference to before, Tony wrote without a thought. Tony's pulmonary embolism was actually a "saddle clot". As I understood it, this was a very large clot blocking both lungs. An additional problem was revealed, thanks to the medical skills of Dr. Brooke Daniel. Tony was found to be allergic to Heparin. He was diagnosed with a condition called Heparin Induced Thrombocytopenia or HIT. This "perfect storm" proved to be no match for our God. That "perfect storm" has also been our "shower of blessings."

God had made Himself known to the multitudes. The God of wonders had stepped into our lives in a mighty way. Word was making its way around. We had visits from some of our fifth floor "medical angel staff", and they wanted to know the details. What a blessing to share! The kids and I lived in the ICU waiting room for about ten days together. I lived there a total of twenty-three, twenty-four days, if you count the night after surgery. A wonderful family adopted me the first night after Tony's surgery. I had the safety and security to rest with these sweet people. My son Derrick spent the night, and day, of his twenty-sixth birthday with me in the waiting room. I left the hospital for a few minutes to go get his favorite birthday meal, sushi, and then I returned. We ate and had our own little celebration in the waiting room. My mom and dad, Roy and Catherine Rollins, would come to get my clothes every couple of days and wash and resupply me. Family and friends kept us supplied with the encouragement of their love and prayers and food. Tony and I lived at the hospital for a grand total of twenty-eight days. When his blood levels were in range, and because of the special blood thinner that he was on, we were actually discharged home from ICU. When it was time, we would go home together. I would not go home without him. I could not leave him.

Social Media-Legacy of Prayer and Faith:

Posted by: Beverly Rollins Dunn – Sept. 20th, 2013 Chattanooga, Tn.

Tony is progressing so well. We are so grateful for the continued support of our family and friends. We continue to hear so much from those who have been a part of Tony's care, and the life changing experience that God put before us all. We are excited to hear now and hope to hear more in the future and some we may never know while here on this earth. We would like to take the opportunity to especially thank our sweet kids that have been standing so wonderfully with us. They have supported us with much prayer, including the leadership of prayer from those little prayer warriors, Kilee, Adelayde, and Elianna. They spent nights and days at the hospital, to be with Tony or support me. A man I spoke with yesterday made a comment, "What a story to tell your grandkids!" I told him they already knew because they helped pray through, by the leadership of a praying moma and daddy. But what a legacy for the generations to come, not only ours, but those who were a witness or heard the news. Thank you sweet Father!!! Please be in prayer for Tony's INR to be 3 or above tomorrow.

Ps 102:18 This will be written for the generation to come, that a people yet to be created may praise the Lord.....NKJV

I became a Christian believer, in Jesus Christ as my Savior, in my mid-teens. I became a "believer" in the summer and fall of 2013. My redeemer is faithful and true! I sought Him and oh how sweetly He came to minister with His great love, power, and compassion. I had never known such closeness to the Father as this. What a blessing is this relationship I have with Him now.

We are so very thankful for the medical team that God worked through. From the beginning of this journey's diagnosis, to our return to our home in the valley and our follow-ups since, we are so overwhelmed with the timing of it all. One of the most awesome things is the way God revealed Himself as He made known His Word in this journey. What a display of God's work as scripture after scripture, even in our social media, was made known. His spoken Word to our hearts......Amen.

My Daughter, Tara Dunn Oakes

Tara, A Daughter's Perspective

My knees buckled beneath me and my body crumpled to the floor, my brother, Justin's words echoing in my head: "Dad is on a ventilator." Never before had I felt such a sense of desperation. Through fiery tears, I cried out to God unlike I had never done before. There was no bargaining. There were no specific requests or promises. Only two words escaped my lips: "JESUS, PLEASE...!!!" For the first time in my thirty years, I understood the scriptures that describe excruciating mourning, sack cloth and ashes kind of mourning. Even now, nearly two years later, my recollection of that moment stirs up an overwhelming flood of emotion. Unbeknownst to me, my life would be forever changed from that moment on.

Needless to say, news of Dad's decline came unexpectedly since his surgical recovery had gone so well to that point. Earlier that day, while walking between classes at UTK, I was surprised to see a missed call from Bev, and immediately I called her back. I could hear a slight tremble in her voice as she shared that Dad's condition had worsened, but she assured me he was in good hands and she would keep me posted. By the end of class, I had heard nothing further and assumed no news was good news. Nevertheless, I headed home to pack my things. I sent a text for an update as soon as I arrived home and within seconds received Justin's call. Once I was able to gather my composure enough to speak, I dialed my soon-to-be husband, Mike, to let him know we needed to leave for Chattanooga. He was somewhat prepared, having been briefed earlier by Bev, and immediately headed my way. We made the ninety-seven mile trip in record time, but it seemed like an eternity—one vast blur of unceasing prayers and tears.

We reached the hospital and ran to the ICU, arriving shortly after Dad's heart had begun beating again. The small private waiting area, that Bev and Justin had been directed to when the code began, was full of familiar faces—family and friends all gathered to pray and offer support— but not a mix commonly seen together. I can only liken the scene to that of a funeral. Even though it was a blessing to be surrounded by so much love and support, it was also a revelation of the true gravity of the situation. The intensity and anxiety was almost tangible, yet I felt an overarching sense of peace envelop me.

We were soon led back through the intensive care unit to Dad's room. I remember an internal conversation where I was attempting to warn myself of what I would soon see, but nothing could have prepared me. The room was full of machines and monitors and unfamiliar sounds. Dad's vitals were far from the normal ranges and a machine was breathing for him. A nurse stood checking the monitors and charting the readings, still shaking her head in disbelief—it was obvious this had been no ordinary code blue. As we entered, she turned, smiled, and confidently said, "This man still has a story to tell! He should not be here right now!" I unsuccessfully attempted to fight back tears, but this time they were not tears of sorrow. Standing by my Dad's side, I was overwhelmed with gratitude that this was not goodbye—God had given us all a Lazarus miracle and another chance.

The next few days were a whirlwind. Every few hours presented a new set of needs and challenges—unstable vitals, fevers, blood clots, dangerously low platelets—which we met with immediate prayer. We kept our social media pages hot by sending out new, specific prayer requests every few hours and the response from family, friends, and total strangers encouraging us and lifting us up in prayer was overwhelming.

With each new worry and fear, God was faithful to provide new glimmers of hope and opportunities to laugh during those darkest of days. We observed one such phenomenon shortly after Dad regained consciousness. Still on the ventilator, he was kept sedated most of the time. They would lighten his sedation as much as possible, during our visits. It was extremely difficult in the beginning to see dad's anxiety as he tried to cope with the new breathing method. His hands remained mitted to prevent him from attempting to remove the tubes while under the confusing fog of sedation, but we would sneak our hands into the mitts so we could hold his. On that day, he raised a mitted hand. When we uncovered his fingers, he was motioning as if writing in the air. I asked if he wanted to write something for us and he nodded in relief. When I asked the nurse for a pen and paper, she gingerly cautioned that due to his sedation, it would be nearly impossible—considering the trauma and sedation—for his brain to communicate well enough with his hand, to be able to write anything, especially legibly. But write he did (in neater penmanship than Justin's by his own admission)! He clearly printed "RINGS". He wanted us to remove his rings, due to the discomfort the swelling in his hands was causing. He followed by writing, "Where am I?" and "How long?" He responded to our answers with raised eyebrows and slight shaking of his head, seemingly wondering where the time had gone. But, most amazingly however, was his response when asked if he knew what had taken place. Not only did he know, but he also perfectly spelled "PULMONARY EMBOLISM".

Social Media-Legacy of Prayer and Faith:

Posted by: Beverly Rollins Dunn – Sept. 22th, 2013 Chattanooga, Tn.

This is day 26 of our journey with Tony. We are still in praise and awe as we continue to greet and talk to all who have been so much a part of our journey at Memorial. We continue to meet ones who had a major part in his care, almost daily, and just to see the joy in them.....brings smiles and tears to me. Every time it is, "you are a miracle". We continue in thanksgiving and praise as we make more

progress toward the door. We are anxious to get home but we are confident, in God's grace, that we are still here because he still needs to be. I told him we would go home together. Our biggest request is that he will increase and maintain his INR (a marker of how well the Coumadin is in his system for blood thinning). We need it to come to at least 3 and not to drop below 2 after drip is discontinued. Please continue to pray for total healing. Praising in the hallway and everywhere, our great Jehovah-Jireh (the Lord will provide).

From the moment dad's heart restarted, we knew, and the prayer warriors surrounding us knew, that without a doubt, God had done something truly, supernaturally, awesome! We received daily reminders of our miracle. During each visitation, we would find doctors, nurses, and other medical personnel, standing at Dad's door or window, watching in awe. Many of them were not even directly involved in his care on the day of the crash, but had heard throughout the hospital. Many of the staff members went out of their way to find us and share their stories of the amazing things they had seen and were continuing to see in him. One day, I received a message from a friend who worked at the hospital and had stopped by dad's room to look in on him. She described walking into his room as if she were stepping into the Holy Spirit. It was a holy experience.....an experience of healing!

A few short weeks after this life-changing event, Mike and I were married. All of our parents were in attendance. I could not have been more grateful, or proud, that my Daddy was able to walk me down the aisle and assist in performing our marriage ceremony. But as blessed as I feel, by each new memory we are able to make as a family, nothing brings me more joy than knowing that God allowed me to witness His unmatched greatness in full force. For me, looking back on this most poignant time in my life, I see clearly that God used this experience to reignite spiritual passions I had allowed to slowly dwindle away. He helped me see the supernatural side of having a close and intimate relationship with Him. He revealed His power in a very real and undeniable way and left me with a new confidence of faith. Through the most treacherous storm of my life, He proved his sovereignty and reminded me there is no limit to what He can do!

My Son, Justin Caleb Dunn

Justin, a Son's Perspective

I was sitting in the office of a potential new client for our first scheduled meeting, and had left my cell phone in the car, which is something I seldom do. It was quite a shock when an employee of the company emerged in the doorway of the company owner's office, interrupting our meeting, and informed me that I had a phone call. The initial embarrassment quickly faded as I received the news from my business partner that Beverly had been trying to reach me to let me know that dad had taken a bad turn, and I needed to come to the hospital immediately. I quickly explained the situation as I excused myself from the meeting and headed to the hospital.

When I arrived at the hospital, Beverly and several others were gathered outside of MICU, where they were treating dad for blood clots in the lungs. A couple of my co-workers had already arrived by that time, to lend their support and prayers. Beverly filled me in on what had transpired and what was being done for dad. It was not long before a physician's assistant came out from the treatment rooms to give us an update on the challenges they were encountering as they attempted to chart a course of treatment to combat the extensive clotting, but we were relieved to hear that we should get to see him at the next MICU visiting hour.

We immediately moved into the MICU once the doors opened only to find the curtain to dad's ICU suite closed. We were met at the entrance of the room and informed that the medical staff was working with him. We would have to wait to see him until someone came to get us from the waiting room. Most of the visiting hour had passed before I was able to return to his room. Dad was sitting up in his bed receiving oxygen through a full-faced pressurized mask. It was obvious his body was laboring to get its needed oxygen, as he drew rapid breaths under the mask. I held his cold hand at the bedside. He seemed focused but peaceful and managed a smile as we shared encouragement and quiet prayers. We were only with him for a few minutes before the physician who was monitoring him, Dr. Steciw, entered the room and stood at the foot of his bed. She watched his cardiac monitor. As the nurse provided the doctor with an update of dad's status her eyes remained trained on the monitor. Unexpectedly, the doctor turned to us and politely, but with a sense of urgency, instructed us that we needed to return to the waiting area. I stood at the door of the ICU for a moment as Beverly held dad's hand, kissed his head, and whispered to him. I told dad that we would be praying. He smiled under the mask and slowly lifted his left hand to give us "thumbs up."

Part of Our MICU Crew
(L-R)Michael Sullivan, Alison Patterson, Theresa
Martin, Kelly Grizzle, and Dr. Richard Pence

Each update was progressively worse, and within a short time we were informed, by the physician's assistant who had been keeping us up-to-speed, that dad was being placed on a ventilator in hopes of relieving some of the strain that his body was under. He was fighting to move enough oxygen through his lungs to overcome the diminished blood flow caused by the saddle clot that had formed in his pulmonary arteries. Many of our family and friends, who had arrived and nearly filled the ICU waiting room, were standing with us to receive the news. As our quiet optimism faded to a new and grave reality, the nervous joking and congenial greetings that we had shared with those who had come to support us had ceased. Terry Rollins, Bev's cousin, put his arms around us there in the hallway next to the courtyard. He comforted us and prayed with confidence. We felt the power of God as many other brothers and sisters in faith answered the call to bombard the courts of the Great Physician with proclamations of healing and restoration.

We fought to hold on to hope as we prayed quietly, but when the physician's assistant came to speak with us a few minutes later we knew immediately that she was not bringing the news we were hoping for. The strained smile that had marked her face for the past couple of hours in an attempt to offer us cautious optimism was gone. She appeared as if she had been laboring and she was fearful as she spoke to us. Dad was not doing well, they were working with him, doing all they could, but we needed to pray. The pain and helplessness overwhelmed us as we moved into a private waiting room. Our next update was from a physician who had been working our code. Beverly asked to be allowed to go back and see dad. She said she had to talk to him. The doctor reluctantly agreed to allow her back but needed a few minutes to "prepare the room" as he put it. Bev asked me if I wanted to go back with her. She assured me it was ok if I did not, but she had to go. Although I knew that I was not prepared for what I might see, I wanted to be with dad, and I did not want her to be alone.

Finally, they came to get us and led us into the MICU room where the code was still in progress. Physicians and nurses were packed into every available inch in the room. Beverly walked through the door and immediately went to the head of the bed. One of the nurses was still on the bed doing chest compressions, in rotation, after nearly half an hour with no success. Dad's eyes were opened and fixed as his body absorbed the continuous force of the compressions. Tear strained eyes throughout the room watched the monitors and hoped for the same miracle that we had been praying for. I have never felt so powerless. I struggled to know how to pray as the grief washed over me. The tears flowed as I worked my way to a space that was opened at the foot of the bed. I raised trembling hands in petition to the heavenly Father to intercede in the life of my dad. There was no sign of life, nothing to give us hope. I watched as those in the room went about doing their jobs. Bev and I left to return to the waiting room where the grieving and the anguish continued to build. Katherine, Beverly's mom, held her as Bev began to sob "I cannot live without him momma". Katherine responded to us with a tenderness and compassion that God bestows only to a righteous mother. Equally impactful was the holy ferocity that she was anointed with as she prayed over us, proclaiming the faithfulness of our God and her unwavering faith in His perfect power, and matchless goodness. She was a rock for both of us in our desperation.

The life altering battle that God had seen fit for us to engage in was raging. I found myself in a fiery trial like I had never ever experienced, but our loving heavenly Father was at work; revealing Himself through His Word, His Spirit, and His people to mold our understanding of His sovereignty, His power, and His unquenchable desire to reconcile the hearts of men and women to Himself. Romans 8:26 came alive to me as I lay across the coffee table in that small room. My weakness was exposed, I did not know what to pray, but the Spirit was pleading my case. My mind was filled with the account of man's beginning—dust, formed by His hand, and brought to life by His very breath. God's Spirit proclaimed that life was not in our tools, our resources, or our knowledge. Only He had the power to create life, has the power to sustain life, and although my dad lay in that ICU room lifeless, He would have the power to reunite us for eternity. From that moment, faith arose to carry me. My prayers were infused with a new fever and confidence in my Savior King that would be my source through the following weeks.

We were soon surrounded by so many who loved us. Each embrace, each prayer of consolation was such a blessing. Looking back at this time, I believe it was one of the pivotal moments that helped to turn the tide through powerful prayers and the love of brothers and sisters in Christ. It was hard to tell the difference between those who were blood relation and those who were not. At that moment we were all a family, as I believe Christ intended for His body to be. We were all grieving and we were all seeking the hand of God in a mighty way.

Several minutes later, we saw Dr. Portera as he came from dad's treatment room. He did not come into the waiting room. Instead, he walked on passed the door of the waiting room on down the hallway. He reappeared a few minutes later and walked on passed again as he went back into the treatment room. A few of us noticed this but was uncertain of what it actually meant, since he had been in the room during the code when Bev and I had gone in to see them working. We would find out sometime later exactly why he had not come in to deliver any news to us. For the time being, we were preparing ourselves. After what Bev and I had witnessed in dad's room earlier, it was hard for us to believe that there would be anything good in the next update. It was the scariest times for us all as we waited.

Eventually, Dr. Portera re-emerged and entered the room slowly. Although dad's condition was grave the doctor reported, "We have a heart-beat." He had a look of disbelief, even confusion. He spoke slowly as if he really did not believe the words that were coming out of his mouth. Watching him was much like the parental experience of listening to a child who is attempting to embellish a story in an attempt to avoid an impending punishment. It appeared as though he was wrestling with the reality of his report. However surreal his words seemed, we were moved by his emotion and concern for our family. We rejoiced at this news, and as I looked around the room, I was overwhelmed with how the power of God had been revealed through all of these who came along beside of us during our hour of desperation.

At that moment, and in countless others in the days to come, I was overcome by how blessed I am to be a child of God, and to be associated with other children of God who truly believe. Many will never experience that supernatural visitation and pure love that can come from the heart of another believer in our Christian community and through the context of pain. This has been one of our most enduring blessings of this journey. "But He knows the way that I take and when He has tested me, I will come forth as gold" Job 23:10 (NIV)

Finally, we were allowed to go back and see dad. We knew he was going to be on a ventilator and closely monitored, but I was shocked to see how many IV pumps, tubes, and monitors surrounded his bed as we walked into the room. Dr. Portera had expressed his concern that dad would likely have severe brain damage after going nearly fifty-five minutes without a heartbeat. He reminded us that his condition was still critical to say the least. The MICU nurse, Alison, was busy making sure that all the life support equipment was functioning and that the cocktail of medications, supporting dad's every life function, were properly adjusted. Sometimes these adjustments were by the minute it seemed. She was not too busy however to look up at us with a smile of assurance. Her expression told it all, she was in a state of amazement. She had been in the room working the code for its entirety. She saw everything from start to finish. Her first words were, "God is not through with this man yet. People do not come back from where he was." This was a statement we would hear from many of the Memorial staff over the next several days as dad slowly re-emerged; one challenge, one set-back, and one subsequent miracle at a time.

I still think back on those difficult days and feel thankful for the spiritual riches we walked out of that hospital with. I would have never volunteered for it, but I would not trade the lessons I learned about the provision of God and the love of His people for anything. I cannot imagine staring down the prospect of losing my father, or spending days on end in the waiting room praying all night for God to give a loved one the strength to make it one more day in spite of insurmountable odds, without the priceless love of God and his people. "Christ died for us so that, whether we are dead or alive when He returns, we can live with Him forever. So encourage each other and build one another up, just as you are already doing. (1 Thessalonians 5:10 NLT)

Chapter Ten

When Love Won't Wait

**Bev's family the Rollins' with Miss Kaye at
our "Gathering of Angels" celebration.**

She opened her eyes to greet yet another day. She gazed through the window to see the dark gray skies above, like so many other days before. Dread filled her mind for she knew what lay ahead. It would be another day of nothing and no one and of the haunting memories of missed opportunities and failures. There were memories of happy times, when love could have made a new direction for her life but at the time was just too confining. She had to be free to pursue her dreams. The dreams were all she could see. Love would wait she thought, but love did not wait and now she was alone, at a time when no one should be alone. She was so afraid.

She thought about her recent roommate and how she had talked about her husband and her children. He had been the strength of her life and had sacrificed and sustained her and her children. He was a wonderful man, she loved him so, but he could not stay. He finally surrendered to the disease that had reduced him to the mere image of what he once was. He left her with an amazing story to tell and to remember, but most of all, he left her with a heart that still overflowed with love. What a treasure! She also talked about the children they had raised, the many accomplishments they had made, and the love they still shared. Almost every day, one of them would show up to set by her bedside and reminisce and laugh and sometimes cry together.

As she looked back on her own life, she would have given anything to know that same kind of love, but she knew she never would. How could she have been so blind? Love did not wait! The love she had witnessed in her roommate was a stake driven through her heart each time she thought of it. In some ways, it was a relief when they came to take her roommate away.

Her sense of depravity and grief has continued. Even now, after she received the news of her roommates passing, she was sure her roommate was not alone when she finally departed! She cried silently. Would anyone be there when she breathed her last? She did not know! Who would care?

She thought about the brief moment in time when there was hope, but she missed the significance. A night of thoughtless pleasure.....she never intended for it to become such a monumental life changing event, but it did! A short time later, she realized that a child was growing in her womb. Then came the choice! Do I allow this to derail all my plans, all my hopes for the future, or do I terminate it in order to pursue my dreams? After all, it is not really a life if I cannot see it or hear it speak.....right? The choice seemed a no brainer at the time. She made it! All of her friends assured her it was the right thing to do, but they quickly abandoned her. They have been absent in her struggle with the emotions and the guilt ever since.

And now, as she lay there in her bed, her mind wondered as it had so many other times. What would life have been like if I had made a different choice? All her answers to this question, in hindsight, led to something far more beautiful. Maybe I wouldn't have gotten to finish my education or even build that fantastic career. I could not have claimed the many successes of achievements through the years. But today, I would not be dying alone. What a terrible price to pay for fleeting success. How sweet it would be to have a loving husband, a daughter or a son, maybe even grandchildren, to hold my hand and share memories and love. I would have become the foundational stone for the building of a life and maybe the lives of many others. I would be surrounded and loved by family. I would not be waiting on love today. I would be loves beneficiary. I would have made an eternal contribution to the good of the world that would live on even after I am gone. How many times has she rolled these scenarios through her mind over the last few years?

She has known for several years how wrong her earlier choices were. She even sought and found help for her troubled spirit. She met God and poured out her soul in repentance. She knew He had heard her prayers, and He had forgiven her. His mercy and grace poured over her like warm oil. She was so comforted in His salvation. But even still, she found it ever so difficult to forgive herself. How can God forgive so easily?

She had committed herself to helping other young women to realize the eternal significance of their decisions and the impact those decisions can have throughout their life. She had shared God with them and taught how He understands the human tendency to yield to deception and pleasures. His mercies are indeed passed our understanding. It is far more important for us to be willing to receive them rather than try to explain them. Let them be our healing!

So she lay there and gazed upward at the darkening skies. She could hear in the next room as a local minister was comforting another patient. Oh how she wished he would come to see her, even though he never had, she prayed oh God please let it be. As the minister was leaving, he walked on passed her door. Her heart sank in disappointment. But then, he reappeared, walking in with a glow and a warm smile. She thought her heart would burst!

Without a word, he took her hand as though he had known her all of her life. She felt the love of God in his touch. God's love did not wait. It was right on time. She was looking up at him as her gaze became distant and the last tear drop formed and rolled down her cheek.

The Bible on her bedside table was open and one particular verse was highlighted in pink. After lifting his hands in prayer, the holy visitor gazed down at it and read these words, "Do not be deceived, God is not mocked, for whatever a man sows, that will he also reap!"(Galatians 6:7 NKJV) He smiled as he pondered over the details of the life that had brushed by him and the glory of the new life she had found. She did not go alone!!

With God, being alone is always our choice. It has never been His intention for us to live separated from Him. Family is His divine gift to us. It is a gift that is meant to soothe and fortify the soul of every child, young or old. Home is the first place we should find God. "Forgive us Lord for what we have made of that gift and for abandoning your plan for experiencing your love."

> "…..It is not good that the man should be
> alone!……" (God) (Genesis 2:18 NKJV)

I remember when I first began to wake up after being deeply sedated and on a respirator for five days. I cannot describe the joy I felt as the images of my wife and children began to become clear. I am not sure if they were actually there when I first awoke or if they had come in a little later. Those first few days seem like a distant dream with most of the details blurry at best. I am certain of how I felt. Knowing they were there was such joy and comfort. I knew something bad had happened, but I had no idea what it was. Eventually, they began to fill me in on the details of the last few days that I had missed. I found their stories to be amazing.

I remember, as I recovered over the next sixteen days in the MICU, how I would lay there looking at the clock. Although I have never been one to be obsessed with time, I found myself longing for time to pass. I was waiting for the next visiting hour. It was not that I was being neglected and needed someone to take care of me. I could not have asked for more compassionate and caring medical professionals to look after me. They showed constant care. They held my hand and talked with me, they prayed with me, and some from the other floors, would come and visit and to talk or pray. My obsession with the clock had more to do with an intimate connection I had with my family.

I had never wanted to be with them in the same way I now found myself wanting to be with them. It is as though God was showing me a treasure He had blessed me with long ago. I had somehow failed to fully appreciate this treasure.

One day in particular, as I waited there clock watching, I had an overwhelmingly sad thought. What if, when visiting hours rolled around, there was no one to darken the doors of my room? What if there was no one waiting a short distance away to come and see me? How devastating would that be? I felt a deep despair at the mere thought of it. I knew that just a few rooms away, my wife and probably some of my children or other family members were waiting. They were there every time that "precious hour" rolled around. They were usually accompanied by other friends….. just icing on the cake.

Social Media-Legacy of Prayer and Faith:

Posted by: Beverly Rollins Dunn – Sept. 23rd, 2013 Chattanooga, Tn.

Headed to our home in the valley. Thank you all and praises to God.

Ps. 46:10 Be still, and know that I am God; NKJV

They sustained me. Their presence made my isolation bearable! I could not imagine going through such a life event without them. I lay there thinking of how many souls depart this world every day and in their last moments are longing for someone to care, someone to touch. And then I ask, why would such an awful scenario even happen? The most logical answer I can come up with is also the most spiritual one.

I heard a statement about business management once, and I think strangely enough it applies to this particular scenario….. "You are perfectly designed to get the results that you get, regardless of whether those results are good or bad!" I believe this was a statement my friend Kirk Wells shared with me. This statement applies to life as well. The final result, and impact of our life, will be the sum total of all the decisions we have made while living it…..whether good or bad. In other words, the decisions we make and the actions we take will determine the outcome, ultimate significance, and contribution of our life.

We rarely consider the long term impact of the choices we choose to make. We make those choices haphazardly. It seems to be the right thing at the time. In reality, every decision we make defines who we are and determines the very course of our lives. God grant us the wisdom to see the future before we do something that will damage all our tomorrows.....

As a young man, I would have done things differently if I had known and could have grasped this truth. In some ways, everyone I love has suffered because of the thoughtless and selfish decisions I made earlier in life. The rebellions of my life have not only affected me, they have affected my children, my spouse, and in some way everyone I love. I now know what God meant when He warned that He would visit the sins of His people on the third and fourth generations. I'm speaking of the long term impact of our sins that we seldom give a thought to. In essence, it was a warning that your sins today will require God's grace upon your offspring. They will be affected for three and four generations. Our actions are far more powerful, with a longer range effect, than most of us have the ability to even comprehend.

I am finally realizing, after all these years, why Jesus was so unrelenting when it came to teaching obedience to the Father, unconditional love, and forgiveness. I am now convinced that abundant life can only be experienced when lived through the lens of true and Godly love. Any deviation or rebellion from God's will is sure to result in absolute loneliness and heartache for many. Obedience and love for God is the only way to live victoriously in this life. To do so will give your children something stable and powerful to build their lives upon. They too will eventually see, and realize, that to build on anything else is only a cheap substitute and will not stand the fire of trial!

Since my release from the hospital, I have had time to review over and again the abundance of the spiritual revelations I have received during, and as a result of, those days. God had a certain purpose for laying me on my back and forcing me to confront the brevity of my life. He indeed had a purpose for taking me to the very threshold of the next life! It has changed me forever.

Social Media-Legacy of Prayer and Faith:

Posted by: Beverly Rollins Dunn – Oct. 14th, 2013 Chattanooga, Tn.

So as our journey continues.....today was our second post-op visit with Dr. Portera. Tony is doing great and they removed his feeding tube. Dr Portera had one of our nurses form the 5th floor come and get us, so we could talk with them for a few minutes. They are great and were all smiles to see Tony walking through the doors with a big smile.....lol. One of them carries a copy of his CT scan from the eventful day, she says she pulls it out and reads it when she is having a hard day and that pulls her through. She said he should not have been breathing at that point. Still feel so blessed to know how God has been good to them, in our journey.....and they give Him all the credit. Continue to pray for them in their work. We left and got on the elevator and Tony and I looked at each other and laughed, as we saw this hanging on the rail in the elevator. God reminds us that His timing is perfect and how funny that we thought He left us a personal note.....lol. And yes God, we do!!!!!

Our Message in the Elevator

People ask me to explain what I saw during those minutes when there was no detectable life in me. Today, my explanation is a simple one. What I saw can only be explained by what I now see. Whatever it was left me with a whole new sense of what is valuable in life. Before all of these things happened, I knew evil was in the world. I can now feel it in the air. It is almost as though I can touch it. I can see it in the actions of the demonically influenced and oppressed. I see it as they work their ungodly deeds. Before, I was tolerant of the atrocities taking place in the world. I am now personally offended and angered by such atrocities. I find it hard to contain my anger! I feel a fire burning deep inside and I know it will eventually consume me. It was not there before, but let it be Lord!!

Being from the south, and in fact having lived my whole life in what many call the "buckle of the Bible belt," my spirit is continually grieved by the things I see happening in our country. Specifically, I see the degradation of our American culture as a result of what I perceive to be the perversion and degradation of the Christian family structure. In fact, this grief is one of the things motivating me to write, and share, what I know is a better way. To me, there is a core root cause contributing to the many of the woes we face in our society today. The issue begins and ends with how we have attempted, through satanic deception, to redefine and restructure the divine concept of church, family, and home. We have in essence, politicized what is, and should have always remained, a spiritual enterprise. Said another way, "we have given heed to seducing spirits and the doctrine of devils."(see 1 Tim. 4:1 NKJV) As a result, the divine purpose of manhood and womanhood have been skewed and brought into odds with each other. The result is the ungodly imposter entities as we are witnessing today, all under the guise of family.

As I parse through the many counterfeit doctrines that have perverted the operation and influence of home and family in our society, I find it an amazing thing that we could have been drawn so far away from the original divine plan. Indeed, this perversion has taken place in America over a period of many years and can be traced back to specific decisions we have made, or allowed to be made as a society. While there is no one person to blame, there have been several individuals who have carried the torch. Those individuals were ignorant of the fact that they were doing the devil's bidding. In their zeal, they planted the seeds that have grown into a force that is bringing our society to the brink of destruction. We as Christians have been witness to it all, yet have done very little to counter it.

First of all, to set the record straight, I am not one of those people who look back to the "good ole days" and wish things were that way again. I am not so naïve as to believe that all things were somehow more perfect then. There has always been sin and a distortion of justice. This is the nature of humanity. I think the major difference between then and now is that we seem to have lost our desire to resist these spiritual temptations and evils. Instead, we are trying to justify our surrender to them, and it is creating a state of empathy and apostasy.

Today's environment makes it safe to be as perverted as you want without apology or accountability. There have always existed sexual deviants, thieves, apostates, politically corrupt politicians, and on and on we could go. However, they had to take far more pains to cover up their deceptions. In a different age, people were far more discerning of evil and far less tolerant of it. To be politically correct, decent people today have been forced to tolerate the most debase of human behaviors. I think what we see today is the function of two conditions. The first condition is the brazen rebellious nature of humanity with a ferocious hatred for God and holiness coming to surface. The second condition is the inability, or unwillingness, of the masses to discern and adequately respond to the dangers this liberal and satanic attitude is most surely creating.

My first thought centers on the denigration of the divine design of the family structure. The distortion on the role of the family, in the maintenance of society and culture, is the place where I feel most of the damage is occurring. There is something that we should all understand about God's design for family. He made the man responsible for the success of the family unit. This has been so misconstrued, misinterpreted, and even abused by men and women through the years. It eventually became the motivational force behind the movement that has attacked, and has attempted to fundamentally destroy, the family structure as it was originally designed.

Man (males) as husband, man as father, man as a stable and loving source of strength and guidance, this was God's original plan. Man, in essence, is the family representative. Man is the ambassador of the home to the greater community of humanity. It was never intended for man to become the ruthless dictator forcing his will upon his family. Instead, he was to be the strong loving guide. He was to provide support and strength to his wife and children so they could fulfill their divine roles and expectations all of which are equally important.

Much of the civil rebellion, we witnessed in the 1960's by women spoke directly to a domestic male dominated abuse of power. Many women were experiencing this abuse from the men in their lives, both husbands and fathers. In essence, their movement was a reaction to a huge failure on the part of many men to balance professional and household responsibilities. The actions taken and the course to which many women were re-directed has produced devastating results in America's homes. A schism was created that has yet to be fully closed and I'm afraid there are powerful political forces at work in our society who do not want to see it closed. These are forces that thrive on division and are enemies of unity.

To quote my very wise granny Williams, "Tony, two wrongs will never make a right!" Granny Williams was so wise. She was always spot on when I needed common-sense spiritual guidance. She knew you could not fix one wrong by doing another wrong. Such an approach will only make matters worse. Yet as a culture, this is exactly what we have done, and continue to do, both politically and morally. That is why we are seeing all of the insanity we are witnessing today. I mention this now because we continue to make this same mistake when dealing with issues today. It seems we want to do the easiest thing which seldom resolves anything. Whether in family circles, political circles, or even religious circles, this approach is a grave mistake. I am convinced that in the world we live in today, doing "right" is very seldom, if ever, the easiest thing to do. It is always the "right" thing to do!

I believe there is an absolute truth. I will always resist this superficial, make up the rules as you go mentality. We are never wiser than the God who created us and who set the boundaries we should be living within. Applying this rule is my first point in trying to understand the spiritual mistake that was made in what became the women's liberation movement in our country.

I was just a young boy the first time I saw the evening news broadcast, in black and white of course, as a group of women were gathered around a huge fire while they burned their bras. I was too young to understand politics and male domination and the like. All I knew was these women, for some strange reason, were burning perfectly good clothing. It did not make much sense to me at the time. It must have been really important, otherwise, why was it on the news? It was many years later when I finally came to understand more about the movement and what exactly they were trying to achieve.

In hindsight, I am asking myself what exactly *was* achieved. How exactly has it impacted or improved our society? I think this is a fair question in keeping with the advice I received from my granny Williams. The plight of women, from a professional perspective, has certainly improved but to what impact on the family unit and the larger society? Was it really the right thing to do or was it one wrong initiative attempting to correct another wrong condition?

That question cannot be answered unless we first know God's divine plan for women. What is their divine role from the home to the greater world community? In reality it is huge! First of all, the myth that God created women out of hindsight to fulfill the needs of a lonely Adam is spiritually ridiculous. God does nothing in hindsight. Scripture says of the animal kingdom that He created them male and female. God knew when He created Adam that the man was an incomplete being. This created man would require a counterpart and a companion. Adam could never have been fruitful and replenished the earth without this special mate.

Eve represented the completion of the creation of man. He was essentially a freak, in that there was no other creature remotely like him..... until Eve. God had created every other animal with a mate and Adam was no different. He needed a mate too. The first man and woman were never intended to compete with each other for dominance or even a paycheck. They were expected to conquer the world together. They were designed to work together in unison using the unique gifts that each had been individually endowed by the Creator. These gifts rightly applied are formidable. They are a mighty fortress in a war torn land. This is still the case today. Unfortunately, we do not get the opportunity to observe it as in times past.

Soon however, disaster struck in paradise. Eve is tempted to disobey the commands of God and she relents. Adam follows suit with Eve and they both find themselves on the wrong side of God for the first time. So what does Adam do? He does what any self-respecting and prideful man would do…..he blames his wife for tempting him! So, here we go. The blame game begins. The first sign of animosity in paradise begins. I would submit to you here that the same spirit which had the power to convince Adam it was all Eve's fault is the same spirit that inspired women to burn their bras in the sixties! The animosities continue. The same spirit that inspired men to dominate their wives and daughters, sometimes cruelly, is the same spirit that drove many wives and young women to rebel against the plight in which they found themselves. What is the real truth? What is God's plan and expectations of His daughters?

The first role of the woman, Eve, was that of a wife. It is appropriate to begin here. I must preface everything that proceeds this statement with a very sobering truth. The truth is this, the relationship between a man and his wife is the most difficult, trying, and sometimes tumultuous of all relationships. The good news…..this is the way it is supposed to be!! Say what? Yes, you heard me correctly.

I believe this truth is one reason why the homosexual lifestyle took root in the world, and specifically in this country. Many observed, as their parents could not cope with the marriage relationship and they themselves suffered when it failed. For a very few of them, but certainly not all, the alternative lifestyle became very attractive. They were duped through their frustration and anger into thinking that somehow this alternative relationship would somehow be easier. For the record, I predict now that homosexual marriage has being forced upon America, we will see skyrocketing divorce rates among homosexuals in the near future. For the record, NO, in my opinion homosexuals are not born that way. They are born sinners like all the rest of us. They make a conscious decision, a choice, NOT TO BELIEVE GOD's WORD. God's Word is very clear on the matter in its original context (not those of some tainted modern day versions). God will hold them accountable for their rebellion, as He will hold all of us accountable for our rebellions. He is no respecter of persons. There is no sin that is special, or exempt, to Him. Political correctness is not in His vocabulary, and never will be.

Marriage is God's way of providing the design for humanity to replenish itself as well as serve for a model for the development of human intimacy. This is what makes homosexual relationships so very abhorrent in the eyes of God. This is why He refers to it as an abomination in the scriptures. By nature, homosexual relationships confuse lust with love. The only fruit the relationship can produce is the satisfying of perverted lust. By the way, many heterosexuals have made the same mistake. Homosexuals are deceived because achieving real intimacy is difficult, regardless of gender, and intimacy is the divine goal of any marriage. I'm afraid they have accepted a false proposition that is propagated by the demonic realm. The real satanic agenda of the homosexual movement is not acceptance or freedom. It is the destruction of the Godly concept and design of family. They are living on a dead end road and want all of us to join them there. Misery loves company. They need prayer and they need to see real and godly love, even if they refuse to recognize it. This kind of love is in short supply in our culture today.

The purification and preparation for all of humanity should begin first in the fires of marriage. Marriage is the trial ground for learning humility and a plethora of other coping skills. Through marriage, we learn to recognize and appreciate the strength of another and the fortitude it can provide in an uncertain life. If two people (Man and Woman) can successfully confront each other's faults, and then help each other to overcome them, they become fit to participate and contribute in the plans of the Creator. Unfortunately at times, hurt feelings and disappointment enter the picture. Instead of helping each other, we get carried away into a caustic "get even" kind of relationship.

I have never forgotten what a Cantor in the local synagogue shared with us as we studied biblical Hebrew one night. He described the relationship of a man with his wife by stating, "A man's wife can and will be his worst enemy and his best friend, both!" I was not really sure how I felt about that, but I have since found it to be true. I have even learned to appreciate it, but I cannot go so far as to say I have always enjoyed it, or even liked it for that matter! My wife's commitment to us, with the fruit it produces, we do enjoy. What a comfort it is to know that she is faithfully committed to our relationship and our family.

The real secret that makes it all work is that my wife has a commitment and a vision to make our home, our children, and our relationship together, absolutely what we and they are intended to be. When I observe her, as she carries on her responsibilities each and every day, it blows me away. She is a modern day version of the Proverbs 31 kind of woman. There is no occupation on earth that demands more, and impacts life in a greater way, than that of a Godly wife and mother. It is a shame that so many young women have been convinced otherwise, or have been forced into a more temporal role in our contemporary society.

Let us now explore the next great and divine role for which women were designed.....the role of motherhood. By nature's very design, it is only women who can fulfill this divine purpose. With all of our intelligence and technologically advanced systems, man has never been able to replicate the human womb and the intricacies of the birthing process. The design is one of the greatest testimonies of the wisdom and power of God. This is His long term care for the sustaining of the human race. But simultaneously, as the institution of marriage came under attack in our society, it would naturally follow that even so would the institution of motherhood. In our new warped and progressive way of thinking, being a wife and mother became the ultimate waste of time and talent. America, and America's children, have suffered from this ungodly deception ever since it occurred.

Please do not misinterpret what I am trying to communicate. Not all women bought into this warped perspective of womanhood. In fact, I think it was only a small minority with a big mouthpiece (wink). The psyche of many women have been troubled and deceived by what in my opinion, is a demonic onslaught. In the broad scheme of things, many women have been left feeling less than significant. Suddenly, being a wife and a mother was not sufficient anymore. Somehow, a woman was no longer complete if she could not prove that she could be successful, in what had traditionally been a man's world.

The most divine of all institutions, the family, of which women are the very epicenter of the universe, became a tarnished concept and made uncertain in their minds. In response, these women have in essence become what I would term super wives and moms! They are competing in the professional world while doing their best to balance and maintain a good healthy home life. Domestically, this is something for which the most well-intentioned male counterpart was unprepared. By all accounts, from what I have witnessed, the female capacity to do this is overwhelmingly amazing! As sincere and capable as their efforts have been, the youth of our nation have still paid a terrible price. Not to blame husband or wife, mother or father, the family unit has been disturbed by the difficulties of the male and female relationship.

In our spiritual service to God, I am afraid many of us take care of ourselves first and then give God the stuff we have left over. I am afraid, as a result our professional pursuits, both men and woman have unwittingly given our children what was left over and sometimes this is not very much. The truth is we are not limitless in our abilities or in the energies we have to invest them. As a result, many children have been forced to resort to alternative means of nurturing and training. Bottom line, the two people who should be most present in their lives are unfortunately absent a large portion of time, if they are there at all.

Parents should be applauded for trying to build a godly home and family. This type of home can only be built through sacrifice. Those who take this responsibility seriously know that rearing successful and godly children is not a part-time endeavor. It requires considerable planning, organization, and implementation to make sure the home unit fulfills our divine purpose and produces offspring that are a blessing and not a burden to our society. This means as parents, we must make it a point to be there. We cannot depend on any other resource to fulfill the role that only we can, and should fulfill. While none of us are perfect, God has given us an indispensable tool to use….. His Love! Love will cover a multitude of our sin, and it will bring peace to our homes, despite the many imperfections we all have.

I am convinced that the feud between men and women, re-emerging in the sixties, has set off an epidemic of other social spiritual issues. These issues are coming to maturity in our contemporary times. Issues such as abortion, homosexuality, sexual perversions in general, pornography, alcohol and drug abuse, violent crimes, materialism, all manner of lawlessness, and the hedonistic mindset run rampant in America. I believe these issues are a direct reflection of a culture that has fallen away from the soundness and stability that was once found and taught in the home.

In truth, even Christians take their children to church in hopes they will learn the truths of God. We fail to take the time to teach them when they are at home. This is a futile exercise! The church was never intended to be a substitute for a Godly home. If we do not live and teach it to our children at home, there will be very little the church can do for them.

My heart hurts for the millions of children who have grown up deprived of the love and the nurturing they should have received from two loving parents. I see them trying desperately to fill the void with so many of the world's substitutes but…..to no avail. I feel their anger when they reach out in violence against others. They think somehow this will bring some amount of satisfaction to their hurting heart…..it does not! There is only more trouble! It is there cry for someone to notice them. They feel all alone.

Today, as Christians look out into our world and our culture, they are appalled at how far away we have drifted from the divine plan. It seems as if moral and spiritual soundness are now more an object of ridicule than an object of desire. Is it because somewhere along the line we allowed our selfish interest to hijack us and lead us off to places we did not need to go? This has caused us to abandon our God given responsibilities in favor of a more selfish existence. Is the anger of today's youth a direct reaction to their abandonment? I think it may be so. The problems we face today are of our own creation. We need to turn around…..and now! It is never too late to start loving. Love will cover a multitude of sins!!

Chapter Eleven

The Journey Continues

Since the beginning of this work more than two years ago, I have found that many of my family and friends need healing for various things in life. I have mentioned friends who have undergone their own trials with the dreaded cancer diagnosis. My friend Barry, who was diagnosed with Sarcoma cancer, is actively trusting God as he battles back. To date, he has been realizing gains and he continues his resistance. My friend Larry, who was initially diagnosed with pancreatic cancer, was then diagnosed with Lymphoma instead. Larry and his wife Becky have seen God do amazing things. Larry is now "cancer clear!" His faith continues to inspire. My mother-in- law Catherine, who stood so strongly in our darkest hour with Bev and our family, has recently been diagnosed with pancreatic cancer and is currently undergoing chemo and radiation treatments. Our hope is that she will eventually undergo the same surgical procedure I had, the Whipple procedure. Her strength and faith continues to be a blessing even as she wages her own war. Please continue to remember and pray for all of these and their families.

These and many others are a constant reminder of how unpredictable life can be. It reminds us how much we are dependent upon the strength and divine care of our heavenly Father and of each other. Please lift up all of the caregivers in prayer. The caregivers need special strength and guidance each day as they attempt to stand in the gap between life and death. Prayer will make all the difference. This week I received word that a dear friend was killed, along with another lady, in an automobile accident in Florida. Death is around us at all times. "God, please keep us as we walk through this valley........"

As I come to the end of this work, it is my prayer that something within these pages has spoken to your heart. It is my hope that something has caused you to take your faith more seriously and to seek the purposes of God in a more meaningful way. I hope that something presented in this work has caused you to re-examine your relationship to God or your lack of relationship, whatever the need may be! I cannot know exactly what the result of this work will be. I have entrusted it into the hands of God Almighty, and it is with prayer I offer it up.

Christians of the world, and especially here in America, are in dire need of an active and powerful faith. We have swiftly moved into the time of apostasy that the Bible has forewarned us about. Those who buy into the satanic doctrines permeating throughout our society will feel the wrath of an Almighty and angry God very soon. Those who resist the demon invasions of our day will feel the wrath and the anger of the god of this world, Satan. This invasion will come from principalities and powers in high places. The god of this world will not stop until he has our allegiance or our destruction. For many, today is a day of decision!

I cannot say, and do not know exactly, why God has chosen to do the things He has done in my life. It is really not for me to question. My purpose is simple. It is to obey as He leads. It is no different than His expectations for all of His other children. I believe that many who read these words will find some of the same awesome truths I have found, except in your own relationship to Him as time moves forward. He is no respecter of persons. He desires to give good things to all of His children.

I could never go so far as to say that God will always provide healing when we ask for it. The truth is that God has deliberate purposes in everything He does. Sometimes sickness and pain, and yes even death, is involved. We should never make the mistake of trying to predict the behavior and the actions of an Almighty God. God answers to no man. Instead, we should be keenly and faithfully aware that He is able to do more than we could possibly ask or imagine. Therefore, you should always ask and prepare yourself for the answer. The answer will certainly come.

Social Media=Legacy of Prayer and Faith:

Posted by: Janna Mann – October 14th, 2013

Tony Dunn talks with Channel 3 about his near-death experience.

MUST READ/WATCH positive news story – I am privileged to work with Beverly Rollins Dunn, a wonderful nurse and follower of God. I believe that God worked a miracle in Tony's life because He knew that He would get all the glory. These two are such a testimony of His faithfulness.

ONLY ON 3: 'Miracle Man' alive and well after heart stops beating for 55 minutes

Posted Oct. 14, 2013 6:19pm

Updated Oct. 15, 2013 6:04am
By Matt Barbour, Weekend Anchor/Reporter

CLEVELAND, TN (WRCB) – A Cleveland man has been dubbed 'the miracle man' by his doctors after his heart stopped beating for almost an hour. He was on the path to recovery after surgery, when things took a turn for the worst. He says he should not be here today but his wife and family are more than thankful he is alive.

Tony Dunn was recovering from major surgery, after doctors found a spot on his pancreas. It was 10 days after the surgery he was set to be released from the hospital but started having trouble breathing. Little did he know that he had a blood clot in both of his lungs and his heart just stopped, for 55 minutes?

"People have asked what I feeling during that time. All I can say Is, Is I felt extremely safe. I felt peace. I felt as though I was in good hands," says Dunn.

Fifty five year old Dunn doesn't remember much during that 55 minutes doctors fought to keep him alive. But he says he does know he was never afraid.

"I don't remember any fear. I don't remember anybody being around that was panicked or anything like that. I just felt extreme peace," he says.

"It was very scary. Very scary," says his wife Beverly Dunn.

For his wife of twenty years, it was the longest hour of her life.....

Since this major event has taken place in my life, I have wondered on many occasions why God chose to intervene the way He did in my medical condition. Was it because of something I have done that merited His grace to such an extent? Was it the power of prayer from my wife and children, Dr. Portera, and all those who carried the fire to His very throne room during those days? Was it to touch the life of a truly wonderful man and physician, Dr. Portera, in order to fulfill His purposes in the lives of family, friends, and medical professionals who needed to experience His presence in a whole new way? My best guess is yes! It was all of these things in some mysterious way and more. It is much more than I can understand or explain. I do know one thing for sure.....the day will come when I feel the peace of heaven once again, but it will be for eternity. It is then I will finally understand. It is then that the understanding will come for us all! Until then.....His will be done on the earth as it is in heaven! Until then, the faithful must keep their eyes fixed on "home". This is the place from which all of our blessings flow. Amen.....

Social Media-Legacy of Prayer and Faith:

Posted by: Beverly Rollins Dunn – Oct. 6ᵗʰ, 2013 Moon Shadows, Tn.

Loving the morning with my sweet husband in his, "healing place" and my "hiding place." Thankful to my sweet Father above for this time. Our journey continues.
I'm not asking you to take away my troubles Lord!

Tara Karis Oakes, Carrie McAmis, Marilyn Harden Gibson, and 61 others like this.

Printed in the United States
By Bookmasters